Tasty Tales

Recipes and Stories from
Peaceful Acres Bed and Breakfast

by Mary Jane Hoober

For Your Information

Proceeds from the sale of this cookbook will be donated to Mennonite Central Committee (MCC) food programs. MCC, a worldwide ministry of Anabaptist churches, shares God's love and compassion for all in the name of Christ by responding to basic human needs and working for peace and justice. MCC provides food assistance for thousands of families every year in situations of disasters, conflict and chronic hunger. In addition to meeting immediate food needs, MCC and its partners also continue to work at solving the root causes of hunger, such as poverty, conflict and inequality. For more information, visit mcc.org.

Tasty Tales
© 2012 by Peaceful Acres Bed and Breakfast
Shipshewana, Indiana

Printed by

Pinch Penny Press

St. Petersburg, FL
727-327-7468
www.pinchpennypress.com

ISBN 978-1-4675-2713-2
9 781467 527132
90000>

Dedication

This book is dedicated to my late husband, Aaron B. Hoober, who always supported me in whatever I chose to do and encouraged me to reach for my goals.

Happy Cooking!
Mary Jane

Acknowledgements

I am grateful to my Lord for His faithfulness and for continually surprising me with inspiration and insights during this project.

Thanks to my daughter-in-law, Carmen, for editing the script.

Thanks to daughter, Kristen, and daughter-in-law, Marla, for testing the recipes and checking them for accuracy.

Thanks to my sons, Lin and Brent and to my son-in-law, Mark, for their support and prayers.

Many thanks to all of my family, friends and guests who were willing to share their recipes and expertise with me through the years.

Table of Contents

Preface

The poet, Muriel Rukeyse, suggests, "The universe is made of stories, not atoms!" I tend to agree with her, as stories are the way we find meaning in life and the way we connect with people. Everyone has a life story and most bed and breakfast guests like to share those stories. Many times sharing our feelings helps to make sense out of the senselessness and chaos in our lives. When there is loss, we are eager to tell what happened before and after the event. We also enjoy sharing our adventuresome and happy times, as well. Verbalizing our stories may bring us to a place of peace as others listen, understand and add insights from their own life's journey. I find that the breakfast table is an ideal place for this to happen. When breakfast is served at 8:00 or 8:30 AM, it is not unusual for guests to be sitting there sharing stories w th each other until 10:30 or 11:00 AM. It is from these times of sharing that the idea for this book was born. Of course, I've changed the names of the guests and I probably don't have all the details exactly correct but the basic happenings are true stories! Our life stories are part of a grand, overarching narrative of God's hand at work in our lives to accomplish His purposes for His good.

In addition to the stories prompting me to work on this book, many people have asked if I don't have a cookbook of the recipes I use for my breakfast dishes. So I decided to combine the two to offer you, "Tasty Tales" Recipes and Stories from Peaceful Acres Bed and Breakfast. My hope is that the stories will give you some laughs and inspiration and that the recipes will satisfy your taste buds!

Background

May 2004

"Hello, Honey, do we have anything planned for tonight? I just made an appointment with the realtor to go see a bed and breakfast near Goshen! I heard about it today and couldn't wait until you were finished at school so I went to see it this afternoon and am eager to see what you think!" Thus began our search for the Bed and Breakfast of our dreams.

I grew up in a Bed and Breakfast in Lancaster County, Pennsylvania. My parents farmed close to Bird-in-Hand when they were first married in 1928. Since a main route ran right near their buildings, they decided to take in overnight tourists which they found to be very enjoyable. Some years later they moved to my mother's homestead near Manheim, Pennsylvania and continued their practice of opening their big, old farmhouse to guests. People came from New York City, Philadelphia and other locations on the East Coast. They were thrilled to come to a farm where they could watch the cows being milked, the field work in progress and take a ride on the tractor or hay wagon. Guests especially enjoyed the fresh fruits and vegetables from the garden, eggs often collected just that morning and meat from our own steers.

As a young girl growing up, I disliked all the work that went along with serving guests. However, as I look back I know that it was a learning experience for me as I discussed religion and politics with guests who were from very different backgrounds than mine. Also, sometimes they had girls my age and we enjoyed getting to know each other. It was a great opportunity to broaden my friendships and learn about other lifestyles and ways of doing things.

My husband, Aaron, was a banker when we got married. He enjoyed meeting people and cared deeply about them so he thought a bed and breakfast was a great idea. Through the years we would occasionally talk about owning a bed and breakfast some day. When it was time to consider retirement, we began thinking more seriously about a bed and breakfast enterprise.

After working with three different realtors, being the highest bidder at an auction but having the owners decide not to let it go for that price, and missing another one because of getting our offer in a few days too late, we found what would become Peaceful Acres while searching the Internet one day.

On a rainy, fall day we decided to drive to Shipshewana to look at the place we saw on the Internet. Well, that was easier said than done as we didn't know anything about the country roads in LaGrange County. There are three different sections of 900 and none of them join! After having been on the other two sections of 900 west and becoming totally frustrated, we called the listing realtor to give us directions. We drove in the short lane only to exclaim that this couldn't be it! It didn't resemble the picture we had seen on the Internet! However, we soon realized that you drive in toward the side of the house but the picture was taken from the front. It didn't take long to figure out that the reason the house was situated that way was so that one would have a gorgeous view from the wrap-around porch and from all of the main rooms of the house. The house is located on 10 acres of woodland with lovely gardens and a meadow in the back of the lot with a small barn. We fell in love with it immediately, especially after viewing the inside and realizing that the layout would work out great for a bed and breakfast.

Then came the challenge of selling our house, negotiating to buy the new house, deciding on renovations and the whole moving process. Choosing an inviting name was another priority. At first we thought of calling it, "Haven of Rest"! However, after receiving negative comments from family and friends about it sounding like a nursing home or a funeral home, we decided on Peaceful Acres. Numerous people tell us that it was appropriately named and that they have chosen to stay here just because of the name. We moved in March of 2005 and began painting, carpeting and adding two bathrooms so that each guest room would have a private bath. Two guest rooms were ready by June; the third by July and the fourth one on the walkout basement level was ready by September. In spite of being the new kid on the block, our first summer was busy. We enjoyed meeting the people from many different places and were privileged to hear their stories and to share their lives with them.

The following March Aaron needed to have hernia surgery. What we anticipated to be common surgery turned out to be a long, serious ordeal! After surgery, he began having severe pain and after much checking and many tests, he was diagnosed with non-Hodgkin's lymphoma. He fought the disease for seven months spending much of that time in the hospital. Unfortunately, the cancer spread throughout his body and he was in much misery and pain. I tried to accommodate

x

some guests during that summer but had to cancel many others. When Aaron was home, he enjoyed relating to the guests who came. Many of them ministered to him and assured him of their prayers. I remember one couple in particular who said, "May we pray with you right now?" That meant so much to both of us to have them pray with us in person. My loving husband went to heaven in October of that year. It was most devastating but I knew my Lord would see me through that time of grief and loss. This was not at all part of our dream of managing a bed and breakfast together.

Family and friends began asking, "What are you going to do with the Bed & Breakfast?" I replied that I would try running it myself with the Lord's help and just take one year at a time to see how it goes. Aaron had told me that I could do it by myself, but my comment to him was that I didn't *want* to do it by myself! We had been so sure that God had led us here for a ministry to others. So my big question was, "Why would God lead us here and then proceed to leave me here alone with all this work to do by myself?" I vividly recall a guest from Branson, Missouri. He wore a large cowboy hat and cowboy boots and had a charismatic personality. He looked at me and said, "Isn't it just wonderful that God led you here when Aaron was still healthy so that he could help you get this place ready for guests? Now you have the bed and breakfast to keep you busy and you have your ministry right here." Of course, he was right but it was a new thought for me. I hadn't been looking at it that way so that was a turning point for me.

I hired my Amish neighbor girls to help as I couldn't take care of the grounds and all the inside work by myself. They are great assistants as are the rest of my neighbors, family and friends who are a wonderful support to me. It is now five years later and I am still here at Peaceful Acres welcoming guests from all around the world. I will continue to do so until the Lord leads me elsewhere.

Mary Jane Hoober

Appetizers

Baked Bananas

1 cup orange juice	2 teaspoons cinnamon
½ cup brown sugar	Dash of nutmeg
1 Tablespoon butter, softened	4 bananas, peeled

Mix first five ingredients in a small saucepan.
Bring to a boil until thickened.
Slice bananas lengthwise and then cut into 1½ to 2-inch chunks.
Place in baking dish and cover with sauce.
Bake at 400 degrees for approximately 5 minutes.

Serves 4

This is attractive served in glass sherbet dishes. Top with a dollop of whipped cream and cinnamon, if desired. I usually serve it as a breakfast dessert.

Baked Grapefruit Strudel

⅓ cup flour	3 Tablespoons butter cut into pieces
¼ cup sugar	2 large grapefruit

Combine flour, sugar and butter in a small bowl.
Mix with pastry blender until mixture becomes coarse crumbs.
Cut grapefruit in half and cut around outside peel and loosen each grapefruit section. Scallop edges. (if you have time!)
Spoon strudel topping on top of each grapefruit half.
Place in baking pan and bake at 400 degrees for 7-10 minutes.

Serves 4.

Garnish with maraschino cherries and a sprig of mint. If mint is not available, I sometimes use a single leaf cut from the top of a pineapple.

Chilled Peach Soup

3   cups chopped, peeled fresh
    peaches (approximately 4
    peaches, depending on their
    size)
1   cup (8 ounce) fat-free plain or
    peach yogurt

1   teaspoon lemon juice
½   teaspoon almond extract
6   Tablespoons sliced almonds,
    toasted
    Fresh mint, optional

In a blender or food processor, combine the first 4 ingredients.
Cover and process until smooth.
Refrigerate until chilled.
Top with toasted almonds and mint.

Serves 4

I usually leave a bit of the red skin on the peaches so it looks appealing and has more color. Guests enjoy this tasty soup and some have commented that it is the first time they have eaten soup for breakfast!

You can substitute any fruit of your choice and use a corresponding yogurt.

French Flan

½ cup sugar (for coating the dishes)
3 large eggs, beaten
⅓ cup sugar
   Pinch of salt

2 cups milk, scalded (heat milk until little bubbles form around the edge of the pan.)
1 Tablespoon flour
½ teaspoon vanilla

Heat sugar in heavy skillet.
Shake skillet and stir until sugar melts to golden brown syrup.
Immediately pour a little into individual custard cups or use a 1½-quart baking dish. Tilt dishes so caramel coats sides.
Beat well remaining ingredients. Pour into prepared dishes.
Set in pan of hot water 1 inch deep.
Bake at 350 degrees for 45 to 50 minutes.
Chill.
Run knife around edges before removing from dishes. Turn upside down on serving plates.

Serves 6
You definitely need a heavy skillet to make this flan because the sugar burns easily. I often find it difficult to coat the sides of the dishes as the melted sugar turns hard very quickly. So it's fine just to have it on the bottom only. This makes a fine breakfast appetizer or dessert.

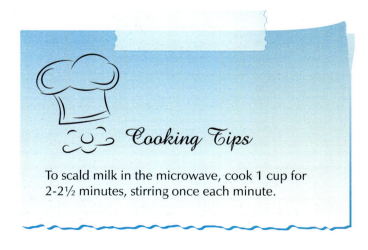

Cooking Tips

To scald milk in the microwave, cook 1 cup for 2-2½ minutes, stirring once each minute.

Frozen Fruit Slush

³/₄ cup sugar
1 cup water
1 sliced banana
1 cup crushed pineapple
1 cup orange juice

2 Tablespoons maraschino cherry
   juice (optional)
6 halved maraschino cherries
   (optional)

Boil sugar and water together.
Let cool.
Stir in remainder of ingredients.
Pour into flat casserole dishes or baking pans.
Freeze.
Thaw at least ½ hour before serving time.
To serve, cut into squares or make dips with large ice cream scoop.
Garnish with orange slice and mint sprig.

Serves 5-6 people

This is another Peaceful Acres favorite. It is especially refreshing on a hot day. It also serves well as a dessert for breakfast or any other time of day.

Breakfast Fruit Salad

To give your fruit salad a new twist, add a can of prepared peach pie filling to your cut pieces of fresh or canned fruit. It makes a good sauce and adds a delicious flavor.

Homemade Granola

2 cups brown sugar	¾ cup chopped walnuts
6 cups regular oatmeal	1 cup oil
2 cups whole wheat flour	2 Tablespoons vanilla
1 cup wheat germ	1 cup water
2 cups coconut	1 teaspoon salt
¾ cup chopped pecans	2 Tablespoons cinnamon

Mix together in large bowl and bake in two 9" x 13" pans at 300 degrees for 1 hour.
Stir every 15 minutes.
Remove from oven and cool on parchment or wax paper before storing.
Keeps well in tight containers for at least a month.

This is a delicious morning cereal served with milk. However, I usually use it in fruit parfaits as an appetizer. I think the only morning I served it as a main dish was the time we were without electricity and I couldn't make anything on the stove or in the oven! I also served fresh fruit, muffins and beverages. It turned out to be a fun morning as we sat and talked by candlelight. Aaron, my late husband, used to make this granola recipe. So we sometimes call it "Grandpa's Granola."

Fruit Parfaits

Layer in goblets or tall glasses:
2 Tablespoons homemade granola
2 Tablespoons your choice of yogurt
2 Tablespoons fresh or canned fruit
Repeat layers

Top with dollop of yogurt, maraschino cherry and sprig of mint. You can save an extra piece of fruit for the top instead of the cherry.

8

Fresh Fruit —Honeydew Boats

Wash the outside of the honeydew melon before slicing it.
Cut honeydew open the long way.
Discard seeds.
Slice in ½ inch pieces from end to end resembling a canoe. (see picture)
Cut melon away from shell and slice into approximately 1 inch chunks still remaining on the shell. Do not cut through the shell.
Add a variety of seasonal fruits such as watermelon, cantaloupe, kiwi, strawberries or fresh pineapple.
Place some in front of honeydew melon boat and some in back.
Add a small dip of homemade lemon or raspberry sherbet, recipe on page 11. (or buy some at the store!)
Garnish with mint sprig and blueberries, if available.

This is a favorite among guests. It is tasty and refreshing!

Homemade Sherbet (to go with fruit boats)

1 – 3 ounce package gelatin of any flavor
1 cup sugar
1 cup water
¼ cup lemon juice (Use lemon juice only if making lemon or lime sherbet. Substitute an extra ¼ cup of water for all other flavors.)
2½ cups milk (I usually use 2% milk)

Combine sugar and water and cook together for 2 minutes.
Pour hot syrup over gelatin.
Stir until gelatin is dissolved.
Add lemon juice (or extra water) and cool.
Add milk and blend together well.
Pour into flat casserole dishes or baking pans and freeze until firm.
Thaw partially and break into chunks with wooden spoon.
Beat with electric mixer or blender until smooth.
Pour into freezer containers and refreeze for later use.

8 servings

Many guests comment about the homemade sherbet. It has a smooth and creamy texture. My daughter tried this recipe with rice milk and reported that it turned out delicious with that substitution. Some people ask if it is a kind of sorbet. It is similar but sorbet is entirely dairy free.

Cooking Tips

To frost grapes for garnish: Dip tiny bunches of grapes into lemon juice; then sprinkle with granulated sugar. Dry on wire rack.

Lemon Cream Parfaits

1/3 cup sugar	2 teaspoons lemon zest
2 Tablespoons cornstarch	2 Tablespoons lemon juice
3/4 cup milk	1/2 cup sour cream
1 egg	strawberries or blueberries

Mix sugar and cornstarch in a small saucepan.
Add milk and whisk until smooth.
Cook over medium heat until it is as thick as paste, stirring constantly.
Remove from heat.
Beat egg and whisk into 1/2 cup of hot mixture.
Pour egg mixture back into the saucepan, whisking well.
Whisk in 2 teaspoons lemon zest and 2 Tablespoons lemon juice.
Cover surface directly with plastic wrap and refrigerate for 1/2 hour.
Stir 1/2 cup sour cream into lemon mixture.
Fill four parfait glasses, alternating berries and mixture.
Chill at least 2 hours before serving.

Serves 4

I prefer chilling this mixture in a bowl and filling the parfait glasses and adding the fruit right before serving time. It can be done either way.

If you use 1% milk and light sour cream, it is a low fat dish. You can also substitute 1/2 cup egg substitute in place of the egg.

Old-Fashioned Egg Custard

3 eggs
½ cup sugar
2 cups milk
1 teaspoon vanilla
Top with cinnamon or coconut

Mix eggs, sugar, milk and vanilla in blender until well blended.
Pour into custard cups and sprinkle cinnamon or coconut on top.
Fill baking pan with ½" water and set filled cups in water.
Bake at 350 degrees for 45 minutes.

Serves 4-5.

I sometimes add a dollop of whipped cream and cinnamon or a
sprig of mint on top.

I use larger stoneware baking cups. If you use smaller cups,
probably 30 minutes baking time is sufficient. If you over bake, it
will be watery instead of smooth and creamy.

*This is an old recipe that my mother made frequently since we
grew up on a dairy and poultry farm. She called it "cup custard".
It is a healthy breakfast dessert that I sometimes serve as a fourth
course. It definitely needs the sugar! One Sunday morning,
because of some responsibilities at church, I left earlier than my
husband. He finished serving breakfast and reported to me that
guests tasted the custard but no one ate very much of it. It then
struck me that I forgot to add the sugar!*

Pears with Raspberry Sauce

Canned or cooked fresh pears, 2 halves per person
½ cup cinnamon applesauce (you can just add a bit of cinnamon to regular applesauce.)

3 Tablespoons of raspberry jelly or jam (I sometimes use whole cranberry sauce instead of the raspberry around the holidays.)

Mix ingredients together, except for pears, and warm in small saucepan.

This is enough sauce for four servings.

Place two pear halves in sherbet or dessert dish.

Add 2-3 Tablespoons of warmed sauce over top of the pears.

Garnish with sprig of mint.

This appetizer is as delicious as it is attractive and so simple to make!

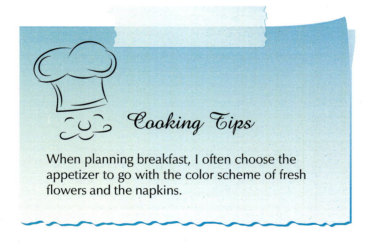

Cooking Tips

When planning breakfast, I often choose the appetizer to go with the color scheme of fresh flowers and the napkins.

By Divine Appointment

One beautiful fall day, Clarissa, her mother, her sister-in-law and her mother rang the doorbell. I could tell immediately that they enjoyed talking and having fun, and that they would be interesting guests to get to know. As we sipped Friendship Tea and ate cookies, we found out more about each other and our families.

The next morning I observed that Clarissa was taking a lot of pictures in different rooms and even outside on the porch. When it was time to eat, she was about to snap a picture of the other three women but I suggested that she get in the picture and I would take one of all four of them. I realized when I took her camera that it wasn't the usual camera that I often see and use. So I told her that I was working on a cookbook and asked if she would take a picture of the plate of food before she began eating. She commented that she has the type of camera that would be used to take pictures for a cookbook. She was quite happy to accommodate me and I immediately noticed that she placed some flowers near the plate and also added a votive candle from the place setting.

The picture turned out lovely and when I complimented her, the others said, "Oh, she is really good. She used to be a professional photographer and has taken the pictures for lots of weddings and other occasions."

Just several weeks before this time, I mentioned to my daughter-in-law that I just don't have time or I forget to take pictures of the food in the morning before I serve it! I said maybe I should just forget the whole idea of publishing a cookbook/storybook. She suggested that I make a lot of the recipes that I plan to use in the book and then hire a professional photographer to come in and take pictures of them. I wasn't sure how that idea would work out but I decided to consider it. Now the Lord had sent me a professional photographer but my mind didn't even compute that fact at the time!

However, when I was cleaning up the kitchen after breakfast, Clarissa sat down at the counter and said, "I'll make a deal with you! I would be glad to come back sometime and take the pictures for your cookbook!" I immediately knew that God had sent her to Peaceful Acres for this very purpose. I was elated and replied that I would be happy to work something out with her. So several months later she spent three days at the Bed and Breakfast taking pictures. It was a fun time of learning to work together and of getting to know each other better. Her friend, Sylvia, came with her to help with lighting and arranging. They were both a great blessing to me.

California Visitors

Teacher friends, Joy and Diane, visited Peaceful Acres together during a school break. Joy and her family had been here the year before and she was eager to share the experience with her friend. We enjoyed connecting about the challenges and rewards of teaching as I had also taught the elementary grades for 24 years. Diane just loved our country Bed and Breakfast, the people and the simple ways of living she observed in Shipshewana. She shared later that she continually asks God why he planted her in California rather than in Indiana.

The next year she brought her husband with her to show him why she loved this area so much. That visit happened to be over the time I was on vacation with my family so my helper, Kathy, served as hostess for Mark and Diane, and the other guests. During that week they became acquainted with Kathy and her family who live nearby. Of course, Diane makes friends wherever she goes. She kept in touch with their family in addition to an Amish carriage driver who took them for a ride downtown. The following year, Diane brought her engaged daughter with her so she could choose a quilt for her wedding gift. Her daughter questioned why she "always" wants to vacation in Indiana!! I recall how fascinating it was for them to watch the lightening bugs, as they had never seen them before. Her daughter began to get a glimpse of the excitement of staying in this rural area.

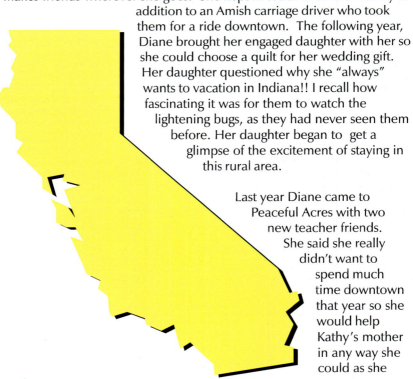

Last year Diane came to Peaceful Acres with two new teacher friends. She said she really didn't want to spend much time downtown that year so she would help Kathy's mother in any way she could as she was in charge of the food for her niece's wedding later that week. When you are serving close to 1,000 people, there is a lot of ordering and picking up to do! On Sunday afternoon Diane and I decided to walk to Kathy's home and discuss our plans for the week with her mother. Diane was so excited to see Richard and Ruth that she not only gave Ruth a big hug but she gave Richard an exuberant hug, too. The look on this Amish preacher's face was priceless as it isn't common for a female to hug a male let alone an English woman with such exuberance. It was all I could do to keep a straight face! Diane had decided that she should not take her gloves off since her fingernails were painted a bright red! That also was rather amusing since it really wasn't even glove-wearing weather!

When Diane picked up Ruth to go shopping the next morning, she told her she had two apologies to make. The first was that she wanted her to know that she was just so happy to see them that she didn't even think that it might not be appropriate to hug Richard. The other was that she was wearing the bright, red fingernail polish because her husband really likes it but she didn't want to offend them. Ruth just laughed and said not to worry about it. She said their young sons did tease Richard about getting a hug after we left the day before. Ruth really appreciated Diane's assistance that week.

The last two times Diane & Company visited, we have had a meal with Richard, Ruth and their six children. Even though their two worlds are vastly different, we always have fun sharing about the food, our families, and our faith. Several times Diane has invited the Amish family to visit her in California. They do like to travel but Richard said he is not eager to visit a big city for a vacation!

I look forward to Diane's visit this summer. I wonder who she will bring with her!

Connecting Cousins

It is not unusual to have sisters or mother/daughter groups gather here for a getaway. They always seem to have so much fun and enjoy their time together. So I encouraged my only sister, who lives 11 hours east in Pennsylvania, that we should plan a yearly time away together. She agreed that it was a good idea! Our first trip was to Branson, Missouri. We had a great time attending concerts and shows and looking around the town. Of course, our time together always includes playing Scrabble and talking and talking!

The next year I suggested that we gather here at Peaceful Acres with our daughters and daughters-in law so that they could all get to know each other better. She thought it was a good idea but questioned whether we could find a time that would fit everyone's schedules. Well, we almost did it! There was only one who couldn't join us but the rest of us had a great time. One came from Florida, several from Pennsylvania, one from Iowa and two of us live in Indiana. It was good for everyone to have a few days away from home to relax and connect. Of course, with two babies under a year old in my family, it gave the cousins time to enjoy little ones, as their children are all older. Everyone was asked to bring several items that would help them share about their families and their lives. It was so interesting to hear about everyone's activities and about their family joys and struggles! Two of my nieces gave us tidbits on "couponing." We also painted Christmas ornaments as our keepsake from the weekend. It was a delight to attend the musical, "The Confession," based on a trilogy of books by Beverly Lewis. We also enjoyed shopping in downtown Shipshewana. Another highlight of the weekend was attending and participating in the youngest grandchild's baby dedication at my son and daughter-in-law's church. It was so special to have family present for that occasion as we usually don't have that privilege.

The weekend went by very rapidly and then for some it was time for the long drive home! I must admit that at first my daughters weren't sure if they were eager to spend a weekend with cousins that they barely knew. However, after experiencing our time together, they were so glad that we had chosen to do that. We made lots of precious memories.

Marriage Proposal

We had just moved into Peaceful Acres and didn't even have things completed yet when Aaron's great nephew, Brady, called to ask a favor. He was visiting his girlfriend in a town close by and they were planning to come to Shipshewana to shop at the famous flea market. He wondered if they could stop by to see us on Wednesday afternoon. We were thrilled to have them visit and invited them to come for lunch. After Aaron gave him directions, Brady asked if we would mind purchasing a dozen tulips for him. Of course, we were glad to do that but I had no idea what he wanted me to do with them. We both wondered about the intent of their visit and how the tulips were connected.

It was so good to see them again and as we visited, I slyly asked Brady to follow me to another room. When I asked him what I should do with the tulips, he excitedly told me that he was planning to propose to Olivia and that tulips were her favorite flower. He wondered if he could put them,

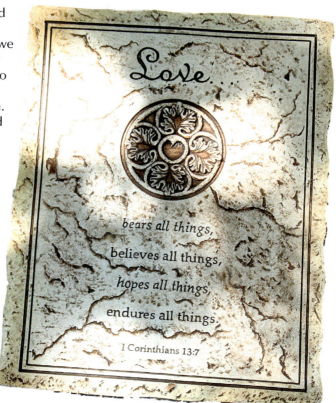

Love...

bears all things,

believes all things,

hopes all things,

endures all things.

I Corinthians 13:7

along with pictures and mementoes he had brought with him, in our most completed room upstairs. However, there was just one problem, he had accidentally left the ring in his backpack at Olivia's parent's home! I told him I had a fake diamond in my scrapbook that was a gag gift at my bridal shower. I agreed to locate the ring and slip it to him! I could sense that Brady was a bit anxious about everything working out just right!

It was a lovely day so we ate lunch on the deck. After lunch, Brady suggested that we take Olivia to show her around the garden area. Of course, he wanted time to set the stage for the big event so he said he would join us shortly. Well, we walked and talked and talked and walked some more and he still didn't show up! Finally, Aaron suggested that possibly Brady didn't know where we were so he would go check on him. Soon they both joined us after which we decided to take a tour of the house. When we got to the room that Brady had all set up, we told Olivia to go in first. Then Aaron and I disappeared! In the midst of all the excitement I realized that the fake ring was still in my pocket. I had never given it to Brady!

Well, Olivia said yes in spite of not having a ring so they were both smiling broadly when they came downstairs! We were so eager to ask why he had chosen to propose at Peaceful Acres. We learned that Olivia just loves Bed and Breakfasts and always has since her grandparents took her to one when she was a little girl. She still dreams of owning and running one of her own someday.

Several years later, Brady and Olivia came back to celebrate their anniversary here.

Pen Pals

There were ten guests at the breakfast table and the conversation was lively as folks became acquainted and shared about their experiences in Shipshewana. I noticed that Bonnie and Jay were rather quiet and weren't contributing much to the conversation. However, when they checked out, they mentioned how much they enjoyed the breakfast time conversation.

Several days later I got a call from Bonnie asking if I would be willing to be her pen pal. She said she thought about just writing to me but then decided she would check with me first. I told her I would be glad to write to her but I wasn't sure how often I would find time to write, especially in the summer.

She already had several pen pals and told me about one in the Shipshewana area. Bonnie had come on a bus tour to this area where they had dinner in an Amish home. Already seated back on the bus after dinner, she felt the Lord telling her to go ask the Amish woman if they could be pen pals. The two of them have been writing to each other for several years now. In fact, when Bonnie and Jay stayed at Peaceful Acres, they had come to the area to visit that pen pal and her family.

Bonnie may not have said much at the breakfast table but she is an excellent letter writer. If it is up to her, letter writing will not become a dying art! Her letters are all beautifully handwritten as she doesn't have a computer and doesn't want one! The letters are usually six or seven pages long and have stickers incorporated here and there to add interest. I have learned about her house, neighborhood, hobbies, family and spiritual journey. Her letters grab your attention and make you want to read on to find out how things turn out! When things don't turn out the way she had hoped, she is still positive. She often shares meaningful Scripture verses to ponder. Even though my letters to her are not as long and probably not as interesting, I am glad that we are pen pals!

Full House

A black pickup truck pulled in the drive on that bright, balmy day making Peaceful Acres show off its very best assets! The young mother came to the front door exclaiming that she just loved this place and would like to spend the night here with her husband and four children. However, they had already reserved a room at a motel downtown and they weren't sure if they could cancel that! As it turned out they could not cancel without paying for the night's stay, so understandably they stayed in town. But they were exploring the countryside for a suitable location for a family gathering later in the summer. Some time later, when Rhoda called me to book the whole house for the family gathering, she casually mentioned that there would probably be 23 of them but quickly explained that some of the teenagers and children would sleep in tents in the back yard. We discussed the logistics of their visit and decided that it could work although I usually say that full capacity is ten guests!

What a delight to meet her husband's parents, their four married children and all the grandchildren. The children spent a long time rolling down the hill in the back yard while the adults spent time connecting and visiting with each other. As darkness approached, they built a fire in the fire ring and spent more quality time together. Before retiring for the night, they all sat in the family room and sang together.
I was in the kitchen doing some advance breakfast preparations so I was privileged to listen to their singing. When they finished with their Good Night song, it reminded me of the goodnight scene from the movie, "The Sound of Music". I didn't have the words to that song until last week when a black truck again pulled in the drive unannounced and the same couple with two little ones wanted a room for the night. I did have a room for them and at breakfast we discussed their family gathering. They gave me the meaningful words to their Good Night Song.

"As now we leave this happy place.
Dear God be Thou our light,
And grant to every soul Thy grace
As here we say goodnight."

Just when I was contemplating writing a vignette about them, they showed up! God was one step ahead of me!

Fiftieth Anniversary Trip

A delightful couple from Germany, accompanied by their daughter, spent eight nights at Peaceful Acres. They intended to stay for ten nights but I couldn't accommodate them the last two nights so I recommended a nearby Bed and Breakfast. Kaiser and Ingrid could speak only a few English words so it was a good experience becoming better acquainted sometimes only through gestures and facial expressions. At other times their daughter, Katrina, who was very fluent in English, would translate for us.

They enjoyed our rural farm area so much; they also live in the country and enjoy gardening and country living. The three of them attended church with me on Sunday morning so during sharing time I introduced them and mentioned that they were celebrating their 50th wedding anniversary. Our associate pastor welcomed and congratulated them in German and everyone clapped in celebration of their anniversary. They were so touched by that expression of kindness. To Katrina's great surprise she met a couple at church that she had bought a quilt from when she lived in the states some years ago.

For an extended stay, it's challenging to serve something different each morning. I remembered that Ingrid especially liked apples so I used various apple dishes several times. They were so appreciative of everything I did for them.

Beverages

Yuletide Wassail

2 cups water (or more)
3 cinnamon sticks
1 teaspoon whole cloves
½ teaspoon ginger
4 cups cider

1 cup pineapple juice
2 quarts cranberry juice
½ cup lemon juice
1 cup sugar

Boil spices and water in large saucepan for 5 – 10 minutes.
Add cider, juices and sugar.
Reheat and serve.
Add lemon or orange slices on top of punch bowl or in each mug.

Wassail is particularly popular in Germanic countries. However, the term itself is a contraction of a Middle English phrase meaning "Be Healthy." It warms you up on a cold winter evening.

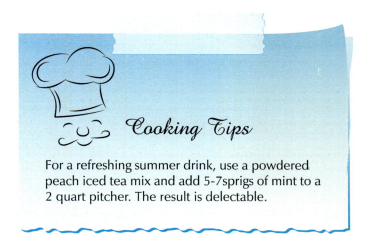

Cooking Tips

For a refreshing summer drink, use a powdered peach iced tea mix and add 5-7sprigs of mint to a 2 quart pitcher. The result is delectable.

Breakfast Fruit Smoothies

2 cups your choice of fruit, fresh
or frozen
1½ cups plain, vanilla or the same
flavor yogurt as your choice of
fruit

1 cup milk
2-4 Tablespoons honey or
sugar

Blend together and serve in juice glasses. Garnish with a sprig of mint.

Makes 6 servings.

This is a nice change from the regular fruit juices served daily. It is especially tasty with blueberries, peaches or strawberries.

Cranberry Tea

7   cups water
¼ teaspoon cinnamon
¼ teaspoon ground allspice
1   quart (4 cups) cranberry juice
½ cup frozen orange juice
     concentrate

¼ teaspoon nutmeg
2   Tablespoons instant tea
1   cup sugar
½ cup lemon juice

Heat and serve.

This recipe is similar to wassail and so simple to put together. I just mix it up in the crock-pot and heat. It is ready to serve to guests in a short time.

Homemade Hot Chocolate Mix

5 cups powdered milk
2 cups instant chocolate mix
1 cup non-dairy creamer
1/3 cup powdered sugar

1 Tablespoon cinnamon
1-4 ounce package instant
   chocolate pudding mix

Mix all ingredients in a large bowl.

This entire recipe will make approximately 35 cups of hot chocolate. However, you can store it in a container for several months and use small portions at a time.

Fill cup with 1/3 cup mix or according to your preference. Add hot water. For a special treat, add marshmallows on top!!

I have had several adult guests who prefer hot chocolate in the morning rather than coffee or tea. Of course, it is a favorite with the children at breakfast.

My grandchildren look forward to drinking it when they come in from sledding in the backyard.

This mixture also makes a nice gift for a friend. I sometimes package this hot chocolate mix to along with a package of the friendship tea mix. (recipe on page 38)

Hot Spiced Cider

½ cup brown sugar	3 cinnamon sticks
1 teaspoon whole allspice	2 quarts apple cider
1 teaspoon whole cloves	Orange wedges (optional)
¼ teaspoon salt	
Dash ground nutmeg	

Combine sugar, allspice, cloves, salt, nutmeg, cinnamon sticks and cider in large saucepan.
Slowly bring to boiling; cover and simmer 20 minutes.
Remove spices.
Serve with clove-studded orange wedge in each mug.

Serves 8

I find this recipe to be more pallet-pleasing than most of the packaged versions of spiced cider. Try it and see which you prefer!

Morning Orange Drink

1 can (6 ounces) frozen orange juice concentrate	⅓ cup sugar
1 cup cold water	1 teaspoon vanilla extract
1 cup milk	10 ice cubes

Combine the first five ingredients in a blender; process at high speed. Add ice cubes, a few at a time, blending until smooth. Serve immediately.

Makes 4-6 servings.

This is a delicious drink but I make it only if there are a few guests as it needs to be served "almost" immediately so I don't make it ahead of time.

36

Friendship Tea

2   cups Tang or dry orange-
    flavored drink mix
1   cup instant lemon tea (if lemon
    flavored tea is not available, I
    use ¾ cup regular instant tea
    and a scant ¼ cup lemon drink
    mix.)

1   cup sugar
1   teaspoon cinnamon
1   teaspoon ground cloves
½ - ¾ cup red hots (optional)

Mix together all ingredients.

Use 4 teaspoons mix per 8-ounce cup or according to your preference.
Pour hot water into cup and stir well.

*Friendship tea makes a great gift for a friend if you package it festively in a
plastic or glass container.*

*I offer this tea to arriving guests in the fall and wintertime. The citrus aroma
and taste makes a warm welcome. We enjoy it along with a variety of cookies.*

Cooking Tips

To create a sugar-rimmed glass for cold drinks,
place juice glasses in freezer overnight. Carefully
dip rim in sugar immediately after taking glasses
out of the freezer.

Feline Lovers

Living along a gravel country road, we seem to attract stray animals, particularly cats. The first cat that adopted me was a small kitten that my neighbor's mother cat decided she didn't want! Feeling sorry for her, I began offering her milk on the deck every day, which she greatly appreciated. I named her Stormy because of her stormy background and because her coloring reminded me of a storm. Stormy was probably about six weeks old when two women, Kristen and Lisa, visited Peaceful Acres. Both being cat lovers, they asked what I was feeding the kitten and where it was sleeping. They seemed to be surprised by my answers that I was feeding it cow's milk and I thought it slept under the deck.

The following evening they returned from their day's adventures rather late. After I went to bed, I heard the deck door opening and closing numerous times. I assumed that they were enjoying playing with Stormy. However, when I went to the kitchen the next morning, I found the whole counter filled with cat paraphernalia! They had bought Stormy a deluxe carrier filled with two plush cushions for cozy sleeping quarters. There was also mother's replacement milk, kitten food, a brush and cat toys. I exclaimed that the cat fairy must have been here last night! They insisted that they didn't want to be

Stormy

paid for any of the items, as it was their contribution to Stormy's welfare. That Christmas my son and daughter-in-law took Stormy to her parent's home where he would have shelter in the barn with the other farm cats.

The following summer my second cat appeared on my front porch just begging to be fed. I noticed that he was an unusual cat with strong, long legs and an extra-long nose. He was quite handsome and was already declawed so I knew he was formerly a house cat. I found out later that he was a Russian Blue cat. I wasn't sure if I wanted to befriend him but after several days some benevolent guests came back from their day's adventures, bringing cat food for him. And so Smokey was here to stay! He loved staying on the front porch and greeting guests as they came up the walk. Folks really enjoyed his company, as he was definitely a "people cat." One couple had at least an hour's photo-shoot with him in the backyard. Smokey was willing to cooperate with whatever poses they desired! As autumn and

Smokey

winter approached, I wasn't sure where Smokey would stay during the cold weather. Fortunately, a frequent visitor from Michigan said her family would take Smokey to join a cat they already had on their small farm. Several months later I received pictures and a newspaper clipping from her telling how Smokey is now involved in pet therapy. Smokey's new owner regularly takes him to a nursing home to bring enjoyment and happiness to the residents there. I'm sure Smokey is thriving under all the attention!

Midnight is my latest adoptee. As you might have surmised, he is pitch black with a small white triangle on his chest and piercing green eyes. He is also declawed and very much wants to live in a house again as I'm assuming he did before. When he first arrived this spring, he was terrified of me and of other cats as a calico cat had appeared this spring, as well. When the calico cat decided to make the neighbors his permanent home, Midnight soon got brave enough to come up on the back porch for food if I wasn't in sight. However, he gradually began to trust me enough to allow me to touch him and was soon interacting with guests, as he loved to be stroked. In the fall, Lin and Sara decided they really liked Midnight and would like to take him home with them if

Midnight

I didn't want to keep him through the winter. When I questioned how they would transport him, they thought he would sit on her lap for the three-hour trip. As I expressed some concern, we decided to put some bedding in a large cardboard box that would become his "carrier" for the trip. They decided they would come back in the afternoon to pick him up.

When they returned, they had bought a halter to keep Midnight from getting away. He was fairly cooperative as we put it on him and Sara was overjoyed as she carried him out toward the car. However, as she neared the car, the cat went crazy, somehow wriggled out of the halter and took off across the meadow. The worst part was that Midnight still had back claws and in Sara's attempt to hold onto him, he scratched up her arm in several places. I was concerned about the scratches. They were concerned about not having Midnight! Several weeks later, I asked my neighbor girl to take him to their barn with the other cats where he would have shelter for the winter. But on the third day he reappeared on the back porch meowing to be fed. So he is still here, weathering out the winter temperatures. He must like it here at Peaceful Acres but he also likes to sit under my bird feeders. I'm not sure what will happen to him in the spring as guests really enjoy watching the birds and I don't want them chased away by Midnight.

Frequent Visitor

Rosie and a friend first visited Peaceful Acres in July of 2007. She decided that it was a good place to bring her Red Hat group so the next year nine wonderful "Red Hatters" descended on our Bed and Breakfast.

The following year only five of them could make the trip and one canceled at the last minute so they invited me to go with them to the Amish home where they usually have supper. Now, having supper with them has become somewhat of a tradition! I have enjoyed getting to know these women so much as we share about our lives. A couple of the women have been widows for many years and one woman's husband died more recently. In addition to sharing our grief journeys, we share about grandchildren, working in various positions in the schools and life in general. There is always a lot of laughter.

Rosie's husband died years ago and the story of her remarriage to her high school sweetheart, Dan, is delightful. Dan's wife had passed away too; so when their children were in high school sports at the same time it gave Rosie and Dan an opportunity to meet up again and become reacquainted. As the saying goes, "The rest is history!" After being here several times Rosie decided to bring her husband for an anniversary celebration. It was great to meet him and I especially enjoyed having them visit my church with me on Sunday morning.

The next group Rosie brought was a group planning their high school reunion. Three of them graduated together and the other two were wives of classmates. This group also had so much fun talking, laughing and playing games together. Rosie is a great Public Relations person. I really should hire her! She will probably receive her free night this year when she makes her tenth visit.

Family Reunion

Julie and Paul had been to Peaceful Acres several times before. However, this time they were entertaining Paul's relatives from the island of Malta. They needed five bedrooms so I offered Julie and Paul the use of my bedroom which I do only occasionally for larger groups. Those accommodations worked well especially for Julie who didn't want to go up and down steps due to the back problems she was experiencing at the time.

I had a small devotional book in my room entitled, "31 Days of Praise" by Ruth Myers. I didn't know that it would become so special to Paul but the Lord knew that it was planted there especially for him. Paul asked me where I had gotten it and wrote down the title, author and publisher so that he could purchase one for himself. When they returned the next year, he said he reads that book every day and it has become a wonderful blessing to him.

Their relatives from Malta were delightful, so appreciative and quite interested in the culture and customs of our area. We had a great time visiting and getting to know each other. One couple wrote the following note in the guest book. "If my uncle and auntie didn't arrange this trip to here in our holiday to the States, our holiday would not be complete to the full. I'm going to miss so much the quiet and peaceful area and house itself. Thanks again and we pray for you everyday. You're an angel from

heaven. For some moments I thought that I was at home in Malta how welcome you have made us!"

They were also a blessing to me and we all had a good laugh together when Paul's brother hugged me before they left. One person commented, "I bet that is the first time you were hugged by a Catholic priest." I believe they were right!

God Chose the Place

That Saturday when Ginny and Reid arrived, I could soon sense that they were in need of some peace and relaxation having come from a large city and stressful jobs. I had barely completed orienting them to the house and the area when Ginny said, "How can we find a Mennonite church to attend tomorrow?" She had been reading about Mennonites and was quite curious about their beliefs, worship services and practices To her great surprise I replied, "I am a Mennonite and I was just about to invite you to attend my church with me tomorrow!" She was overjoyed and was sure that God had led them here to Peaceful Acres. That was the start of a lasting friendship.

The couple has continued to come to Peaceful Acres for refreshment once or twice a year. In fact, they are the first couple to have received their complimentary stay as the tenth visit is on the house. We can always pick up just where we left off last time and reconnect as good friends. Reid especially appreciates the wireless Internet connection as he can easily keep in touch with business partners back home. We also keep in touch by sharing prayer requests with each other. They have been able to attend church services with me several times since that first experience. On their last visit we decided to visit the Amish-Mennonite Church located close to Peaceful Acres. Another couple staying here went with us, as well. The folks there were so warm and welcoming to us so it was a great experience.

On one visit we built a campfire in the fire ring on a crisp fall evening We all had a great time with the other guests but especially enjoyed showing the couple from South Korea how to toast marshmallows and turn them into delicious s'mores. We shared stories and laughed together late into the evening.

When they visited last year, they were just two weeks away from their due date of the arrival of their first child! They had checked out the hospitals in the area so they knew which ones would take their insurance and Ginny had bought her packed suitcase for her hospital stay just in case the baby arrived early! My son and daughter-in-law and their family were visiting at the time. They had a new baby daughter so my daughter-in-law was able to give Ginny some helpful tips and allay some of her fears that concern any first time mother! I have also had the privilege of visiting them in their home.

Guest Author

Upon my return from Pennsylvania where I was visiting our oldest son and his family, I discovered that the renowned author, Beverly Lewis, was coming to Shipshewana to do a book signing at the Christian bookstore there. The date was only about one week away so I quickly called my friend in Pennsylvania, who is also a friend and consultant of Beverly's, to ask how I should contact Beverly to invite her to stay at Peaceful Acres. She suggested that I email her immediately which is what I did. I invited her to stay overnight or to come for breakfast or just for tea. I explained that if her schedule was full, I would come to the store to meet her. The very next day she replied to thank me for the invitation and explained that her schedule was quite full and that her manager had already made plans for their overnight stay. She did say that if she could fit a short visit into her schedule, she would contact me the day before. I did not hear from her the day before so I assumed that I would go to the store to meet her. To my surprise, my phone rang at about 8:15 the next morning.

The caller said, "This is Beverly Lewis and I am traveling with my manager and my editor. We were wondering if it is still okay if we stop in for breakfast this morning." Of course, I was delighted to answer that it was just fine. I figured that the menu I was serving for my other guests would be fine for them, as well. My only disappointment was that the guests who were here were not acquainted with

Beverly as an author so they decided not to wait for an hour to eat breakfast with her at a later time. Many of my guests discuss her Amish novels over breakfast and would have been so excited to meet her. However, I had a delightful time having breakfast with Beverly and her manager and editor. They enjoyed touring the bed and breakfast and Beverly commented that she would like to come back with her husband sometime. I was wondering if that would ever happen but my Pennsylvania friend told me that if she mentioned it, she would probably do that sometime. In my mind, I somehow compared her last-minute visit with Christ's second coming! I thought about what I would have changed if I had more advanced notice. The only thing I could think of was that I would have had her books in a more visible space!

I am pleased to tell you that she did return with not only her husband but with her daughter and granddaughter, two aunts and an uncle. They all stayed at Peaceful Acres for the opening weekend of the musical, "The Confession," which is adapted from three of her novels. This new musical was presented at the Blue Gate Theater in downtown Shipshewana. It was a joy to see her again and to meet her family. It was truly a weekend to remember.

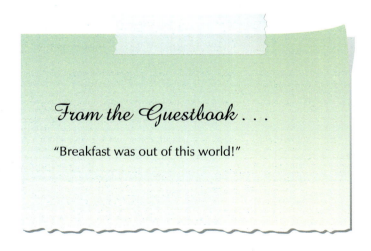

From the Guestbook . . .

"Breakfast was out of this world!"

Hospitable Guests

It was a bright, sunny June afternoon when sisters, Jean and Marian, their sister-in-law, Sylvia and friend Linda arrived at Peaceful Acres. I could immediately tell that they were fun-loving and gregarious.

Soon after they had checked in, a lovely older couple, Sam and Erma, arrived and checked into the Garden Getaway Suite which is the only room on the lower level. The outside entrance to that room can be used instead of coming in the front door and using the inside stairway. I noticed that Sam and Erma preferred to use the outside entrance and stayed to themselves most of the time which is fine since that is what some guests are seeking.

That night the four ladies asked me to join them to play games. We had a great time playing Split Second, Catch Phrase and Apples to Apples. We all laughed so hard while playing that the glass dishes in the curio cabinet rattled!

I wondered how the conversation at breakfast would go with the vivacious ladies and the reserved couple. To my surprise the ladies got

Peaceful Acres Bed and Breakfast

Sam and Erma to join in the conversation and everyone really seemed to be enjoying themselves both mornings. The third morning it was Jean, Marian, Sylvia and Linda with some new guests at the breakfast table since Sam and Erma had left the previous day. I always dislike when the phone rings around 8 o'clock just when I am ready to serve breakfast but that is what happened that particular morning. To my surprise I heard Erma's voice saying, "Would you please tell the four ladies that we really miss them this morning? It is boring with just Sam and me looking at each other across the breakfast table and we aren't even having a gourmet breakfast!" I knew then that they had certainly felt welcomed and included by my cheerful new friends.

After breakfast, one of the ladies shared about her personal struggles which was quite an inspiration and encouragement to me. Many times God has sent people here by divine appointment to be a blessing to me. Each guest has a unique gift to offer each other and to me. I will never forget the wonderful care basket these ladies sent to me after my husband went to heaven. Included was a "memory candle" which still shines in his memory on my kitchen windowsill.

Recently, two of the ladies, along with their husbands, returned to spend another getaway time at Peaceful Acres.

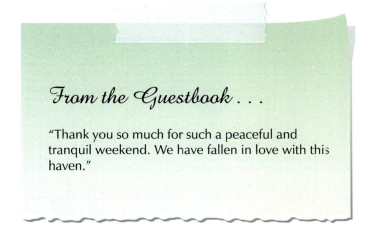

From the Guestbook . . .

"Thank you so much for such a peaceful and tranquil weekend. We have fallen in love with this haven."

Lasting Friendship

Jared and Ella's first visit was for their anniversary celebration. They had two young children at the time so it was their getaway weekend without children. They enjoyed their time here and later that year Ella came by herself for a mom's getaway. She wanted to spend the time meditating, reading and walking for exercise. I didn't realize that she had gone out the downstairs patio door and walked downtown which is approximately a three-mile walk. I became quite concerned about her when she didn't come upstairs any time after breakfast. I knew she hadn't had lunch but I thought maybe she was just resting and I didn't want to bother her. I was relieved when I saw her walking in the lane later in the afternoon. Jared was supposed to take his getaway sometime in the future. However, on Ella's second night Jared found some friends to keep the children and showed up here to surprise her!

On a family getaway to Peaceful Acres, I can picture Ella and their oldest child, Amanda, sitting at the dinette table doing school work as Ella was home schooling her for Kindergarten that year. I recall them enjoying the trails through the woods and swinging on the tree swing in the back yard.

Then in 2009 they announced that the Lord was leading them to return to their home area near their families in Oregon. I knew I would miss their visits! However, I was pleased to see Ella, their son, Matthew, and their new baby later that year when they traveled to the area with Ella's mother who had come to attend a conference in Michigan.

We do keep in touch via email and facebook but to my surprise the whole family came to stay at Peaceful Acres again this past summer. They decided to come back to the area where they had lived to attend a family church camp and to visit friends. I was so pleased to be included in their travels. We always have a good time reconnecting when they visit and have so much in common as we share about our lives and spiritual journeys. I still have a lovely silk flower magnet on my refrigerator door that Amanda made for me at camp. It reminds me to pray for their family. Since being in the Bed and Breakfast business, I feel like I have gained some additional children and grandchildren!

Breads, Muffins and More

Apple Pumpkin Streusel Muffins

2½ cups flour
2 cups sugar
1 Tablespoon pumpkin pie spice
1 teaspoon baking soda
½ teaspoon salt

2 eggs, lightly beaten
1 cup mashed pumpkin
½ cup vegetable oil
2 cups peeled, finely chopped
   apples

Streusel Topping

2 Tablespoons flour
¼ cup sugar
½ teaspoon cinnamon
Cut in 4 teaspoons butter until mixture is crumbly.

Combine flour, sugar, pumpkin pie spice, baking soda and salt.
Set aside.
Combine eggs, pumpkin and oil.
Add liquid ingredients to dry ingredients.
Stir just until moistened.
Stir in apples.
Spoon batter into greased or paper-lined muffin cups, filling ¾ full.
Sprinkle streusel topping over batter.
Bake at 350 degrees for 35-40 minutes.

Makes 18-20 muffins.

These muffins are a favorite of my grandsons and guests like them too. They are a good addition to a fall menu.

Cooking Tips

One can often shorten the baking
time for muffins so they don't dry out.

Cappuccino Muffins

2   cups flour
¾   cup sugar
2½ teaspoon baking powder
1   teaspoon cinnamon
½   teaspoon salt
1   cup milk
2   Tablespoons instant coffee
     granules

½   cup melted butter or margarine
1   egg
1   teaspoon vanilla
¾   cup mini semi-sweet chocolate
     chips

Combine flour, sugar, baking powder, cinnamon and salt.
In another bowl, stir milk and coffee granules until the coffee is
dissolved.
Add butter, egg and vanilla; mix well.
Stir into dry ingredients just until moistened.
Fold in chocolate chips.
Fill greased or paper-lined muffin cups ⅔ full.
Bake at 375 degrees for 17 to 20 minutes or until muffin test done.
Cool for 5 minutes before removing from pans to wire racks.
Makes 14 muffins.
Serve with espresso spread.

Espresso Spread:

4   ounces cream cheese, cubed
1   Tablespoon sugar
½   teaspoon instant coffee granules
½   teaspoon vanilla extract
¼   cup mini semi-chocolate chips

Combine all spread ingredients; cover and refrigerate until serving time.
Makes 1 cup spread.

*I recently had a guest ask if this recipe will be in the cookbook. I said it would
so I had to make sure it made "the cut." The special spread makes these muffins
extra tasty.*

Zucchini-Banana Bread

Cream together:
½ cup butter or butter-flavored shortening
1 cup sugar
½ cup brown sugar

Add:
2 beaten eggs
1 teaspoon vanilla
1 cup grated zucchini
2 medium bananas, mashed
2 cups flour
½ teaspoon baking soda
½ teaspoon salt
2 teaspoons baking powder
½ cup chopped nuts

Mix well.
Pour into greased loaf pan.
Bake at 350 degrees for one hour.
Cool on rack for approximately 20 minutes before taking out of pan.
Cool completely before slicing.

Makes one large loaf.

This bread is moist and tasty! Add spreads as desired.

Caramel-Banana Muffins

½ cup chopped pecans
2 Tablespoons sugar
1 teaspoon cinnamon
1 3-ounce package cream
cheese, softened
⅔ cup sugar
1 egg
1 medium banana, peeled and
mashed (½ cup)
1 teaspoon vanilla

1¼ cups all-purpose flour
¾ teaspoon baking powder
¼ teaspoon baking soda
¼ teaspoon salt
2 Tablespoons caramel-flavored
ice cream topping
1 Tablespoon butter, melted
1 medium banana, peeled and
thinly sliced (optional)

Line 12, 2½-inch muffin cups or six jumbo cups (3¼ inch) with paper or baking spray.

Toss together the pecans, 2 Tablespoons sugar and 1 teaspoon cinnamon.

Combine cream cheese, butter and ⅔ cup sugar with mixer until well blended.

Add the egg and beat well.

Beat in the mashed banana and vanilla until mixture is combined.

Stir together the flour, baking powder, baking soda and salt.

Add to the banana mixture, beating on low speed until just comined.

Stir in ¼ cup of the pecan mixture.

Spoon half the batter into prepared muffin cups.

Drizzle ½ teaspoon caramel topping over batter in each cup.

Top with remaining batter.

Drizzle each muffin with a little melted butter and sprinkle with remaining pecan mixture. If desired, top each muffin with additional slices of banana and drizzle with caramel topping just prior to serving.

Bake at 375 degrees for 18-20 minutes (22-24 minutes for jumbo size) or until an inserted toothpick comes out clean.

Makes 12 standard or 6 jumbo muffins.

I recently acquired this recipe and found it to be pleasing to the taste buds and appealing in appearance.

Cinnamon Rolls

1 package yeast (2¼ teaspoons)	**FILLING:**
¼ cup warm water	¼ cup butter, softened
1 cup warm milk	¼ cup sugar
¼ cup butter	¼ cup brown sugar
¼ cup sugar	2 Tablespoons cinnamon
1 teaspoon salt	2 Tablespoons light corn syrup
1 egg, beaten	
4 cups bread/baking flour (may need a bit less flour)	

Dissolve yeast in warm water.

Combine milk, butter, sugar and salt.

Add dissolved yeast and 1 cup flour. Mix well.

Add egg and mix again.

Add remaining flour and stir until combined. Do not knead. Dough will be soft.

Let rise until double. Punch down and roll out into a 10" x 12" rectangle.

Spread with filling. Roll up rectangle jellyroll fashion.

Slice in 1" slices and put in greased 9" x 13" pan or two 9" round cake pans.

Let rise until double.

Bake at 350 degrees for 20 to 25 minutes.

FROSTING:

2 ounces cream cheese, softened	1⅓ cups powdered sugar
2 Tablespoons butter, softened	1 Tablespoon milk
½ teaspoon vanilla	

Combine cream cheese and butter. Add remaining ingredients and beat until smooth. Frost while rolls are warm.

Makes 1 dozen rolls.

These cinnamon rolls are a bit different with the cinnamon filling and the cream cheese in the frosting. They are easy to make and have always turned out well. They need to be put in the freezer unless you are using them within 24 hours. Heat rolls in the microwave before serving.

Festive Cranberry Bread

5 cups flour	2 eggs
2½ cups sugar	2 cups orange juice
1 teaspoon baking soda	½ cup butter, melted
3 teaspoons baking powder	1 cup water
2 teaspoons salt	2 cups fresh or frozen cranberries

Combine first five ingredients.
Make a well in center of dry ingredients.
Add eggs, orange juice, butter and water.
Whisk until combined.
Fold in cranberries last.

Pour into 3 greased and floured loaf pans.
Bake at 325 degrees for 1 hour.

Makes 3 loaves.

This is a colorful bread to serve around the holidays. Serve with cinnamon butter. (Recipe on page 62.)

Upside Down Pineapple Muffins

1 can (20 oz.) crushed pineapple	1 package yellow, lemon or
⅓ cup margarine or butter, melted	pineapple-flavored cake mix
⅔ cup packed brown sugar	

Drain pineapple; reserve juice.
Stir together melted margarine and brown sugar.
Evenly divide sugar mixture into greased muffin cups.
Spoon pineapple over sugar mixture.
Prepare cake mix according to package directions, replacing water with reserved pineapple juice.
Evenly pour batter into muffin cups.
Bake at 350 degrees for 20-25 minutes or until toothpick inserted in center comes out clean.
Cool 5 minutes. Loosen edges and invert onto serving platter.

Makes 21-24 muffins.

I often freeze them in a tight container and reheat them before serving. Add a cherry on top for added color and appeal.

Fruit Cocktail Coffee Cake

1½ cups sugar
2   eggs
½   cup vegetable oil
2   cups flour

2   teaspoons baking soda
½   teaspoon salt
1 –15 ounce can fruit cocktail, including
    liquid

Blend and mix ingredients.
Pour into a 9" x 13" pan.
Bake at 350 degrees for 45 minutes.

Topping

½   cup margarine or butter
¾   cup sugar
½   cup evaporated milk (I often
    use regular milk)

1   teaspoon vanilla
¾   cup chopped nuts (optional)

Combine margarine, sugar and milk in saucepan.
Bring to a boil. Boil hard for 1 minute.
Remove from heat.
Add vanilla and nuts.
Pour over hot cake.

*I have used this recipe for 40 some years. It was given to my late husband,
Aaron, by a colleague when he was a banker in Pennsylvania. It was one of his
favorite cakes because it is so moist and flavorful.*

Cooking Tips

Muffins will be moister if you grease the
muffin tins instead of using cupcake
papers.

Lemon Yogurt Bread

3 cups flour	3 eggs
1 teaspoon salt	1 cup vegetable oil
1 teaspoon baking soda	1¾ cups sugar
½ teaspoon baking powder	2 cups lemon yogurt
1 cup finely ground almonds	1 Tablespoon lemon extract

Topping (optional)

¼ cup sugar
Juice of 2 lemons

Mix together the flour, salt, baking soda and baking powder.
Stir in nuts and set aside.
Beat eggs, then add oil and sugar; beat well.
Mix the lemon extract into the lemon yogurt.
Add the flour mixture to the egg mixture alternately with lemon yogurt, ending with yogurt.

Spoon into 2 greased and floured loaf pans or a 10-inch bundt pan.
Bake at 325 degrees for 50-60 minutes, or until done.
Cool "briefly" in pans on rack. While cooling, make the glaze by combining the sugar and lemon juice. Mix well. Make glaze just before using or it will not be smooth.
Turn out of pans and poke holes in top of loaves with a fork.
Slowly spoon the topping over the loaves.
Let cool completely before slicing.
Makes two loaves.

This bread is suitable either for breakfast or for afternoon tea. It has a light, delicate lemon flavor and a fine texture. It freezes well.

Lemon Curd (excellent spread for scones and breads)

1 cup fresh-squeezed lemon juice (approximately 6 lemons)	2 cups sugar
	½ cup butter
7 Tablespoons grated lemon zest	8 eggs, lightly beaten

Combine lemon juice, zest, sugar and butter in top of double boiler. Heat, stirring, until sugar is dissolved and all ingredients are smooth. Add lightly beaten eggs to the lemon mixture and whisk together. Continue cooking, whisking constantly, until mixture is thick. Remove from heat; pour into sterilized jars, cool and store in refrigerator.

Makes 5 cups.

My daughter-in-law introduced me to lemon curd that you can buy at the grocery store. It is quite tasty and a lifesaver when you are short on time!

Cinnamon Butter (Delicious with breads and scones)

½ cup butter, softened
2 teaspoons cinnamon
¼ cup powdered sugar

Mix ingredients together with mixer.
Store in container with lid.
Keeps in refrigerator for at least one month.

I was first served this tasty butter when my daughter-in-law invited her mother and me to a very special Mother's Day Tea. The hostess was willing to share her recipe with us.

Oatmeal Coffee Cake

1 ½ cups boiling water
1 cup quick or regular oats
Mix boiling water and oatmeal and let stand 20 minutes.

Cream together:
½ cup margarine or butter, softened
3/4 cup brown sugar
3/4 cup granulated sugar
½ teaspoon vanilla

Add:
2 eggs
1 ½ cups flour
½ teaspoon salt
1 teaspoon cinnamon
1 teaspoon baking soda
oatmeal mixture

Mix well.
Pour into greased 9" x 13" pan.
Bake at 350 degrees for 30 minutes.

Topping

Melt 6 Tablespoons margarine or butter in small saucepan.
Add:
¾ Tablespoon cream or milk
¾ cup brown sugar
1 cup chopped nuts of your choice

Mix together and spread over hot cake.
Broil several minutes until topping bubbles. Watch carefully so it doesn't burn.

Many guests are surprised to learn that this coffeecake contains oatmeal. It is moist and goes great with coffee or tea.

Melt in Your Mouth Biscuits

(Delicious served with Sausage-Apple gravy, recipe on page 107)

2 cups flour	2 Tablespoons sugar
2 teaspoons baking powder	½ cup vegetable oil
½ teaspoon cream of tartar	1 egg
½ teaspoon salt	⅔ cup milk

Mix above ingredients. (don't over mix!)
Drop by heaping teaspoonful on baking sheet or bake in greased muffin tins. Make tins about 2/3 full.
Bake at 375 degrees for 20 minutes.
Makes 12-13 biscuits.

I searched far and wide for a good biscuit recipe and finally found it next door from my neighbor.

Morning Glory Muffins

6 eggs	4 cups grated carrots
4 teaspoons vanilla	2 cups raisins
2 cups vegetable oil	1 cup chopped nuts (I usually use
2½ cups sugar	½ cup pecans and ½ cup
4 teaspoons baking soda	walnuts)
4 teaspoons cinnamon	1 cup coconut
1 teaspoon salt	2 apples, grated (any variety)
	4¼ cups flour

Beat eggs.
Add vanilla and oil and mix well.
Mix in all remaining ingredients.
Pour into greased muffin tins.
Bake at 350 degrees for 20 minutes.

Makes approximately 36 muffins.

These muffins were a popular item at the Trolley Café, the restaurant we formerly owned in Goshen. Guests at Peaceful Acres like them, too. They are moist and good for you! Enjoy!

Peach Coffee Cake

Topping
¼ cup melted butter
½ cup flour
½ cup sugar
Dash cinnamon
Combine above ingredients until crumbly. Set aside. If you mix the topping first, it will crumble better when sprinkling over batter.

Cake
1 box yellow or lemon cake mix
1 – 21 ounce can peach pie filling
3 eggs, beaten

Combine cake mix, pie filling and eggs by mixing gently with a spoon. It is fine to have some smaller lumps remaining. I like to cut the peach slices in half so there are more pieces in the cake.
Pour into greased 9" x 13" pan.
Sprinkle topping over batter.
Sprinkle a small amount of cinnamon-sugar on top of crumbs. (optional)
Bake at 350 degrees for 30 minutes or until golden.

This is so easy and delicious! It is especially yummy when warmed slightly. If you're serving it for a dessert, add a dollop of whipped cream.

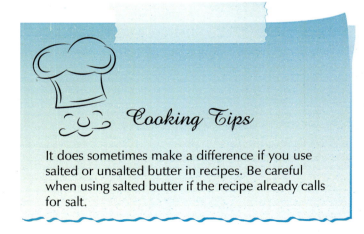

Cooking Tips

It does sometimes make a difference if you use salted or unsalted butter in recipes. Be careful when using salted butter if the recipe already calls for salt.

Rhubarb Muffins

Combine thoroughly:
2½ cups flour (can use half whole wheat flour)
1   teaspoon baking soda
1   teaspoon baking powder
½ teaspoon salt

In separate bowl, mix well -
1   cup buttermilk (you can substitute sour milk or plain yogurt)
¾ cup brown sugar
½ cup oil
1   egg, beaten
2   teaspoons vanilla

Stir dry ingredients into liquid mixture until just moistened.

Stir in 1½ cups diced rhubarb
½ cup chopped nuts

Fill greased muffin cups ⅔ full.
Top with the following crumb mixture:

¼ cup sugar
1   Tablespoon melted butter
1   teaspoon cinnamon
1   teaspoon flour

Bake at 375 degrees for 20 minutes.

Makes 18 muffins.

I like to use seasonal ingredients so this is a popular recipe for springtime guests. My rhubarb is the most beautiful and the tallest it has ever been this spring thanks to my kind neighbor who put horse manure on it a few months ago! Yes, I do wash it thoroughly!

Scrumptious Scones

2 cups unbleached flour (I use baking flour)
1 slightly heaping Tablespoon baking powder
2 heaping Tablespoons sugar
1 teaspoon salt
5 Tablespoons chilled, unsalted butter, cut into chunks
1 cup half and half (do not substitute regular milk)
1 cup fresh or frozen fruit, chopped and tossed in flour. (Leave
blueberries and raspberries whole.) You can use a combination of
chocolate, butterscotch, peanut butter or cinnamon chips, nuts,
coconut, almond flavoring or dried fruits. I found that mini-chocolate
chips and coconut is a tasty combination, as well as, dried cherries,
coconut and almond flavoring.
Be creative!

Mix flour, baking powder, salt and sugar in medium bowl.
Cut in butter with pastry blender until just mixed.
Make a well and pour in half and half. Fold in just to incorporate.
Fold in fruit. Do not over mix!
Press into a 8" by 12" rectangle. Brush with half and half and sprinkle
with coarse sugar.
Cut rectangle into four pieces. Cut pieces again on the diagonal into
triangle shapes.
Grease or use parchment paper on baking sheet.
Bake at 350 degrees for 15 to 20 minutes until browned on top.
Cool on rack.
Do not cover with plastic wrap!
Can be reheated before serving.

Makes approximately 12 scones depending on how large you cut them.

*Scones are a small Scottish quick bread often served with tea. A guest who sold
these popular scones at her café shared this recipe with me. I learned that a
scone recipe without eggs makes them more moist and flavorful.*

*Serve scones with lemon curd or cinnamon butter. The recipes for spreads are
on page 62 .*

Observant People

It is interesting to hear people comment about the various things they notice. I think one of the most unusual observations was the lady who was quite excited about the hearts on the toilet paper. The brand I often use has tiny hearts and flowers in a quilted pattern on it. I just buy it at any store that sells toilet paper. She was so sure that it was something quite special that I needed to order and couldn't imagine how I found such unique toilet paper for my bed and breakfast!

There is another heart at Peaceful Acres, which I hadn't even noticed. One guest commented that it was so special to have a heart-shaped stone right by the front steps where you come in. I didn't know what she was referring to so I went outside to look. Yes, right there beside the front steps is a lovely heart-shaped stone. It isn't difficult to recognize the shape immediately! However, I had never noticed it before! The guests surmised that it was a gift for me sent from heaven by my late husband. What a pleasant thought!

Recently a guest commented on the light fixture in the sitting room. It has always been there but I don't remember anyone else being as fascinated with it as this person was! The globe has Victorian-style designs with dancing ladies on it. It came from the ballroom of the tallest building in downtown Elkhart, Indiana. Our church mission agency, where my late husband used to work, had their offices on the second floor of that building. When the building was renovated, evidentially some of those fixtures were made available for buying or for the taking. We received this light globe at a white elephant gift exchange at an office party. We kept it for many years thinking that we would sometime find a good place for it. I recall my husband questioning if we should use it but after it was in place, we both agreed that it had found a good home.

Another item that I remember someone being excited about is the toilet paper holder in the main floor bathroom. I have utilized an old granite potty, which I found in my parent's attic, to hold an extra roll of toilet paper! It was probably the very potty my parents used to train me! One woman came out of the bathroom calling to her husband, "Honey, you just must come see this!" She was so captivated by the idea and was eager to do something similar in her bathroom back home.

WELCOME

Enter as strangers...

Leave as Friends

71

Hershey Descendant

Cousins, Marla and Audrey planned to meet here at Peaceful Acres as it was a halfway destination for both of them. Marla arrived first. She immediately noticed the booklet entitled, "Milton S. Hershey" in my antique Hershey cupboard in the entrance. She excitedly asked about its significance and was even more excited to find out that I am a fifth cousin of Milton S. Hershey, the founder of Hershey Chocolate factory in Hershey, Pennsylvania. Marla was a third grade teacher and taught a chocolate unit each year in her classroom. She thought her students would be so amazed to know that she slept in the house of a Milton Hershey ancestor. I added that another interesting fact is that my mother always told us that the farmhouse where we grew up in Manheim, Pennsylvania was built on the same blueprint as the Hershey Homestead in Hershey.

Marla and Audrey continued to meet here at Peaceful Acres every summer. They would sit in the sitting room for hours, talking about their family history and their present-day lives. On another trip, Marla brought her college roommate and then she and her husband came to visit last fall.

One summer I gave her a special Hershey tin filled with chocolates for her students and fellow teachers. Her students wrote me delightful thank you letters full of lots of questions about Indiana, chocolate and my relationship to the Hersheys. I had fun answering all their questions and included chocolate facts for their interest. For example, did you

Hershey/Kreider Homestead in Manheim, Pennsylvania.

know that Hershey kisses are one of the most popular candies in the United States? Also, a popular theory on how they were named "kiss" is that they were named for the sound or motion of the chocolate being deposited during the manufacturing process. I also told them a story about my Grandpa Hershey who originally owned the farm where I grew up. The Hershey factory sent him train carloads of broken chocolate pieces, which he fed to his hogs. He had prize-winning Hampshire hogs so possibly it was the chocolate that made his hogs sturdy and handsome!

One year Marla wrote the following email when she returned home. "I arrived home at around three o'clock this afternoon. I can't thank you enough for allowing us to stay in your beautiful home. I stopped to see my mother after I returned to tell her all about my visit with Audrey and my stay at Peaceful Acres. She actually commented on how calm and peaceful I seemed. I truly received a new sense of well-being and contentment –that sounds kind of "hokey" but I really did!"

I enjoyed getting to know Marla and Audrey over the years and we have become good friends.

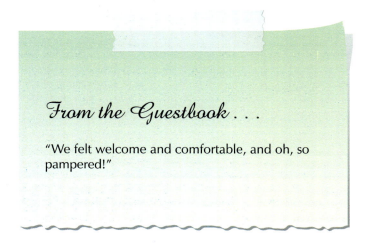

From the Guestbook . . .

"We felt welcome and comfortable, and oh, so pampered!"

Inspiring Visit

Jaci and her two daughters chose Peaceful Acres as their destination for their annual adventure to celebrate her daughters' birthdays. She had traveled to Shipshewana only once before with her daughter's Junior High School field trip. They loved it then and decided many years later to return to Shipshewana to celebrate birthdays. Jaci's daughters are now married and she is blessed with three grandchildren. Since Jaci and her daughters enjoy the homey atmosphere and coziness of a Bed and Breakfast, they searched the internet for an inviting place to stay. After their visit here, they wrote that Peaceful Acres is their favorite Bed and Breakfast!

Jaci enjoys writing devotionals for the ladies in her Bible study group at her church. Her dream is to publish these meditations in a devotional book some day. The following is a devotional she wrote after visiting Peaceful Acres.

"My daughters and I took a mini vacation and while on this vacation, we stayed at a countryside bed and breakfast. As we pulled up to the house and saw the beautiful landscaping and flowers as far as your eyes could see, it took our breath away. When walking into the house we heard a voice saying, "Come in and make yourself at home."

The next morning we were blessed with an outstanding, candlelit breakfast. After our breakfast was served, we were talking and discovered that our wonderful hostess is a Christian. She told us that she and her husband bought the Bed and Breakfast four years ago. They spend a lot of time getting it ready for guests and making the house and grounds beautiful. After their work on the house was finished and ready for guests, her husband went to be with the Lord.

Now you might read this and question why God would take her husband after they worked so hard to finish their bed and breakfast. But when she told her story the first thing my daughters and I thought about was that God had a purpose for her husband. He was to prepare a beautiful place for his wife before he was called home. This was a gift from God. It was a place where Mary Jane could look around and see the wonderful memories of her loving husband. God, through her husband, prepared a place for her.

Our loving God prepared a beautiful home for Mary Jane through her husband but imagine what a wonderful home He is preparing for us when we go to our heavenly home. It says in John 14:2, "In my Father's house are many rooms; if it were not so, I would have told you. I am going there to prepare a place for you." Oh, what a wonderful home that will be!"

Dear Heavenly Father,
Thank you for taking care of us and thank you for preparing our Heavenly home.

Written by Jaci Cox

I praise the Lord for several guests who gave me this insight into my mission at Peaceful Acres. I also want to thank Him for His faithfulness and for preparing a home for us in heaven.

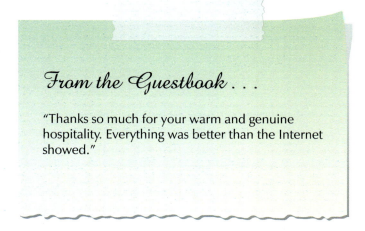

From the Guestbook . . .

"Thanks so much for your warm and genuine hospitality. Everything was better than the Internet showed."

"Enter As Strangers, Leave as Friends"

The first time Joe, Susan and their ten-year old Alexis arrived at Peaceful Acres, Alexis was not sure that she would enjoy staying at someone else's house. After all, there was no swimming pool or gym area in which to play! However, after her first visit, she was sold on staying at a bed and breakfast and was eager to accompany her parents to stay here the following year, and every year thereafter. It didn't take us long to realize that first year that we would become good friends. They enjoyed visiting with both Aaron and me as we had so much in common, in addition to being brothers and sisters in Christ. Alexis would have her nose in a good book when we were engaged in long discussions.

The second summer they came to Peaceful Acres, Aaron was in the hospital battling cancer. Of course, they wanted to go visit him and it was an encounter I will not forget. Joe could barely talk because he was overcome with emotion seeing Aaron in that condition! I knew how much he cared about him.

Their family usually stays almost a week and they say they are still not finished exploring Shipshewana and the surrounding areas. Their interests are varied and they enjoy the handmade crafts, antiques and the history of the area. They sometimes buy relics for the antique booth they maintain in their home area. Often they meet relatives here to experience Shipshewana together!

I eagerly anticipate their visit and to tasting the homemade goodies they so graciously shower upon me. Now Alexis is sixteen and she still looks forward to their yearly visit! Last year they even included a college visit to check it out for future reference!

It's a Small World

About eighty years ago a Hungarian author, Frigyes Karinthy, wrote a story in which he suggested that any two individuals in the world are connected through five acquaintances. Of course, it's an unproven theory but there is a dynamic at work that links us to others: The providence of God is working through His Word to accomplish His will. Thus, I don't believe these connections are chance meetings!

A business appointment about an hour from Peaceful Acres is what prompted two brothers to call for reservations. They knew their wives would enjoy exploring Shipshewana while they were gone. The couple from an eastern state had to wait quite a while for the other coup e from southern Indiana to arrive as they had snowy roads to navigate.

As I visited with the first couple, I discovered that he was involved in a large poultry business. Since my family has a large poultry operation in Pennsylvania, I thought he might have heard of their business. As it turned out, he had interviewed with my nephew for a job and had played golf with him. He commented, "Out of all the Bed and Breakfast establishments I could have chosen, I picked this one!" We were both amazed at the coincidence. However, I don't think it was just a coincidence. I pray that God will send specific people here who will bless me and that I will also be a blessing to them.

It's a Small World (2)

I remember pulling over to the side of the highway when my cell phone rang while traveling through Iowa. The caller, who was from Pennsylvania, wanted to make a reservation at Peaceful Acres for the coming summer. He told me they have a Bed and Breakfast in Pennsylvania Amish Country and they were eager to visit Amish Country in Indiana.

Originally from New York, they traveled to Lancaster County frequently to stay at their favorite Bed and Breakfast there. When they retired, they bought a house at a scenic location to open their own Bed and Breakfast. When I told him I was originally from Pennsylvania, we began making connections. I discovered that they live just a mile down the road from one of my best friends in Pennsylvania. They had no idea that I knew their neighbor and church friend when they called to make their reservation. When I visited our mutual friend in Pennsylvania, we went to see them and toured their lovely Bed and Breakfast where we enjoyed sharing stories and recipes.

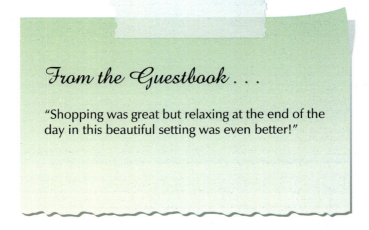

From the Guestbook . . .

"Shopping was great but relaxing at the end of the day in this beautiful setting was even better!"

It's a Small World (3)

I was privileged to have an interesting young couple, who were on furlough from their mission assignment, stay at Peaceful Acres. The other guests at the breakfast table enjoyed hearing about their work with the blind in Haiti.

The couple left a prayer card with me, which was posted on my refrigerator as a reminder to pray for them. Several months later another guest was so surprised to see the prayer card there. This guest, a college professor, had the missionary as a student in some of his college classes. They had kept in touch with them throughout their lives. However, neither couple knew that they had both chosen to stay at Peaceful Acres.

The missionary couple had stayed in the Harvest Room, which has a wheat theme. So this Christmas they sent me a lovely handmade scarf with wheat embroidery stitched by a Haitian woman who participates in one of their self-help projects. It was a welcome and beautiful addition to the Harvest Room.

From the Guestbook . . .

"There is a chorus of birds and the air smells so fresh – so much to take in. We loved watching all the creatures."

Cookies

Apple Brownies

²/₃ cup butter
2 cups brown sugar
2 eggs
1 teaspoon vanilla
2 cups flour

2 teaspoons baking powder
¼ teaspoon salt
1 cup peeled, chopped apples
½ cup chopped walnuts
  Powdered sugar

Cream butter and sugar.
Add eggs and vanilla and mix well.
Add flour, baking powder and salt. Stir well.
Stir in apples and nuts.
Spread in well-greased 9" x 13" pan.
Bake at 350 degrees for 30-35 minutes.
Cool and sprinkle with powdered sugar.

Makes 36 bars.

These soft brownies are a delicious variation of the regular chocolate brownies. They make an attractive presentation if you mix the light-colored apple brownies and chocolate mint brownies (recipe on page 86) on your serving plate.

Amish Sugar Cookies

3½ cups flour
1   teaspoon baking powder
1   teaspoon baking soda
1   teaspoon nutmeg
1   teaspoon salt
1½ cups margarine (no substitutes!)

2   cups white sugar
1   teaspoon vanilla
1   teaspoon almond extract
2   eggs, slightly beaten
1   cup sour cream
    Sugar for garnish

Stir together flour, baking powder, baking soda, nutmeg, and salt.
Beat margarine, sugar, vanilla and almond extracts until creamy.
Add eggs and sour cream
Beat well.
Gradually add flour mixture, beating well.
Line cookie sheets with parchment paper.
Drop 2" apart with medium-sized cookie scoop.
Sprinkle with sugar.
Bake at 375 degrees for 10-15 minutes or until set.
Don't let them get too golden.
Remove from cookie sheet and place on cooling rack.
Store between wax paper.

Makes approximately 5 dozen.

A room mother shared this recipe with me when I was teaching first grade. I remember how much the students enjoyed these cookies as a special treat. They are also a favorite of my grandchildren. A soft, yummy cookie for any age! They make very attractive holiday cookies by adding colored sugar on top.

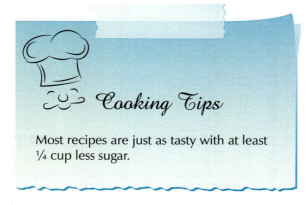

Cooking Tips

Most recipes are just as tasty with at least
¼ cup less sugar.

Chocolate Mint Brownies

1   cup flour
½   cup butter or margarine, softened
½   teaspoon salt
4   eggs
1   teaspoon vanilla
1 – 16 ounce can chocolate-flavored syrup
1   cup sugar

Filling

2   cups powdered sugar
½   cup butter or margarine, softened
1   Tablespoon water
½   teaspoon mint extract
3   drops green food coloring

Topping

1 – 10 ounce package mint chocolate chips
9   Tablespoons butter or margarine

Combine the first seven ingredients in a large mixing bowl; beat at medium speed for 3 minutes.
Pour batter into a greased 9" x 13" baking pan.
Bake at 350 degrees for 30 minutes
(top of brownies will still appear wet.)
Cool completely.
Combine filling ingredients in a medium mixing bowl; beat until creamy.
Spread over cooled brownies. Refrigerate until set.
For topping, melt chocolate chips and butter over low heat in a small saucepan.
Let cool for 30 minutes or until lukewarm, stirring occasionally.
Spread over filling. Chill before cutting.
Store in the refrigerator.

Makes 4 to 5 dozen.

The mint filling not only makes these brownies attractive but quite tasty. Do not let the top layer chill too long before cutting them as it is difficult not to crack the chocolate if it is too cold and hard.

Cinnamon Favorites

½ cup butter	1 teaspoon baking powder
1 cup sugar	¼ teaspoon salt
1 egg	½ cup chopped nuts
1 teaspoon vanilla	1 Tablespoon cinnamon
1¼ cups flour	1 Tablespoon sugar

Cream together butter and sugar.
Add egg and vanilla. Beat well.
Add flour, baking powder and salt to creamed mixture. Chill.
Mix together nuts, cinnamon and 1 Tablespoon of sugar.
Roll dough into balls and roll in nut mixture. Do not flatten balls or grease your cookie sheets.
Bake at 350 degrees for 12-15 minutes.

Makes approximately 2 dozen cookies.

This crisp, cinnamon-flavored cookie is a favorite among guests. It is very similar to the classic Snickerdoodle cookie recipes. It was shared with me by my sister-in-law early in our marriage.

Coconut-Blueberry Cheesecake Bars

½ cup butter
¾ cup finely crushed graham
    crackers
½ cup all-purpose flour
½ cup flaked coconut
½ cup ground pecans
¼ cup sugar

12 ounces cream cheese, softened
⅔ cup sugar
4 eggs
1 Tablespoon milk
1 teaspoon vanilla
2 cups fresh blueberries

Lightly grease 9" 13" baking pan; set aside.
For crust, in small saucepan heat butter over medium heat until the color of light brown sugar. Remove from heat; set aside.
In medium bowl stir together graham cracker crumbs, flour, coconut, pecans, and ¼ cup sugar. Stir in butter until combined.
Evenly press on bottom of prepared pan.
Bake at 350 degrees for 8-10 minutes or until lightly browned.
Meanwhile, in large mixing bowl beat cream cheese and ⅔ cup sugar at medium speed until combined.
Add eggs, milk and vanilla. Beat until combined.
Pour over hot crust. Sprinkle blueberries on top.
Bake at 350 degrees for 18-20 minutes or until center appears set. Cool in pan on rack. Cover and refrigerate.
Cut into bars. Store, covered, in refrigerator.

Makes 32 bars.

These bars are so tasty. When blueberry season is here, I pull out this recipe. I am blessed to have a you-pick blueberry patch at neighbors nearby. I am doubly blessed to have the option of them picking the blueberries for me if I don't find time to pick them myself. They are delicious served with a variety of cookies for afternoon tea or I have also added them to the baked goods offered at breakfast.

Coffee Bars

1 cup raisins	2 eggs, beaten
1 cup coffee (a good way to use leftover coffee)	1½ cups flour
½ teaspoon cinnamon	½ teaspoon salt
⅔ cup shortening	½ teaspoon soda
1 cup sugar	½ teaspoon baking powder

Mix together raisins, coffee and cinnamon. Set aside.
Cream together shortening and sugar.
Add remainder of ingredients to sugar mixture.
Add raisins, coffee and cinnamon mixture.
Mix well.
Bake in greased 8" x 12" baking pan.
Bake at 350 degrees for 20 to 25 minutes.
While bars are still warm, glaze with the following mixture:

Glaze

2 Tablespoons coffee
1 cup powdered sugar

Makes 24 bars.

These bars are delicious served with hot or cold drinks. They can be used as a snack or as baked goods for breakfast.

I remember coming home from a doctor's appointment one day the summer my husband was ill. I was questioning what kind of baked goods I would serve my guests for breakfast the next morning and felt too exhausted to do any baking. Then I found a tray of these coffee bars on my kitchen counter. The Lord had sent them to me via a kind neighbor.

Double Chocolate Cookies

2¼ cups flour
1   teaspoon baking soda
1   cup butter or margarine,
    softened
¼   cup sugar
¾   cup light brown sugar, firmly
    packed

1 - 4 ounce package instant
    chocolate pudding
1   teaspoon vanilla
2   eggs
1 – 12 ounce package chocolate
    chips
1   cup chopped nuts (optional)

Mix flour with baking soda.
Combine butter, sugars, pudding mix and vanilla in large bowl.
Beat until smooth and creamy.
Add eggs, and then gradually add flour mixture.
Stir in chocolate chips and nuts. Batter will be stiff.
Drop by rounded teaspoons onto ungreased cookie sheets or covered
with parchment paper.
Bake at 375 degrees for 8 – 10 minutes.

Makes 3 ½ to 4 dozen cookies.

*These cookies are great to satisfy your chocolate cravings! It is easy to over
bake these cookies so I usually bake them at 350 degrees!*

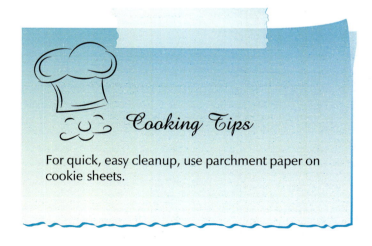

Cooking Tips

For quick, easy cleanup, use parchment paper on
cookie sheets.

Frosted Banana Bars

½ cup butter or margarine,
   softened
2 cups sugar
3 eggs
1½ cups mashed bananas
   (approximately 3 medium-
   sized bananas)

1 teaspoon vanilla
2 cups flour
1 teaspoon baking soda
   Pinch of salt

Cream butter and sugar.
Beat in eggs, bananas and vanilla.
Combine flour, baking soda and salt.
Add to creamed mixture and mix well.
Pour into greased 10" x 15" pan.
Bake at 350 degrees for 25 minutes. Cool.

Frosting

½ cup butter or margarine, softened
1 8-ounce package cream cheese
2 cups powdered sugar
2 teaspoons vanilla

Cream together butter and cream cheese.
Add sugar and vanilla. Beat well.
Spread over bars.

Makes 36 bars.

This recipe is a great way to use up those overripe bananas. The bars are moist and full of flavor.

Holstein Cookies

1	cup butter	4	teaspoons baking soda
1	cup shortening	1½	packages instant vanilla pudding
¾	cup white sugar		
2¾	cups brown sugar	1½	packages instant chocolate pudding
8	eggs		
4	teaspoons vanilla		Chocolate chips (optional)
8	cups flour		

Mix butter, shortening, sugars, eggs, vanilla, flour and baking soda in a large bowl.
Divide dough into halves and add vanilla pudding to one bowl and chocolate pudding to the other.
Add chocolate chips to one or both bowls if you desire.
Take half of each color and roll into ball.
Flatten with palm of hand.
Bake at 375 degrees for 8 minutes.

Makes 8 dozen.

This recipe, among others, was shared with me by a wonderful baker, my Amish neighbor friend. The original recipe called for 16 eggs, 16 cups of flour, etc. I cut the recipe down to half of those amounts. I find it easy to use a medium-sized cookie scoop and fill it with half vanilla and half chocolate. These cookies are unique in appearance and taste great! They are black and white almost like a Holstein cow!

Lemon Cake Cookies

1   white cake mix
1   lemon cake mix
4   eggs
2/3   cup oil
¼   cup flour
    Powdered sugar

Mix above ingredients with mixer.
Roll dough into small balls.
Roll into powdered sugar and press on greased pans.
Sprinkle additional powdered sugar on top.
Bake at 350 degrees for approximately 13 minutes.

Makes approximately 2 ½ dozen cookies.

These cookies are so simple to make but so delicious. People often request this recipe.

Oreo Truffles

1 – 8 ounce package cream cheese, softened
1 – 1 pound, 2 ounce package of Oreo cookies, finely crushed (about 4¼ cups, divided)
2 packages (8 squares each) semi-sweet chocolate, melted

Mix cream cheese and 3 cups cookie crumbs until well blended.
Shape into 48 (1 inch) balls.
Dip in melted chocolate; place on waxed paper-covered baking sheet.
Sprinkle with remaining cookie crumbs.
Refrigerate 1 hour or until firm.

Makes 4 dozen.

Mixing the cookie crumbs with the cream cheese makes these truffles taste like they have a fudge filling in the center. They are easy to make and disappear fast on a cookie tray.

Lemon Curd Bars

1   cup butter, softened
1   cup sugar
2   cups flour
½ teaspoon baking powder
1   10-12 ounce jar lemon curd (or make your own from recipe on page 62.)

⅔ cup flaked coconut
½ cup slivered or sliced almonds or coarsely chopped pecans, toasted

Line a 9" x 13" baking pan with foil, leaving about 1 inch of foil extending over the ends of pan. Grease foil, set pan aside.
In a large bowl beat butter with mixer for 30 seconds.
Add sugar; beat until combined.
Add flour and baking powder; beat until just combined and mixture resembles coarse crumbs.
Reserve ⅔ cup of the crumb mixture; set aside.
Press remaining crumb mixture evenly into the bottom of the prepared pan.
Bake at 375 degrees for 5-8 minutes or until top is golden.
Remove from oven. Spread lemon curd over hot crust to within l/2 inch of the edges of pan.
In a medium bowl stir together reserved crumb mixture, coconut, and almonds.
Sprinkle crumb mixture over lemon curd.
Bake at 375 degrees for 18 – 20 minutes or until edges are golden and topping is brown.
Cool in pan on a wire rack.
Remove baked mixture from pan using the foil to lift it out.
Place on cutting board; cut into bars. Store, covered, in the refrigerator.

Makes 32 bars.

These bars are more "lemony" than the usual lemon bars. The coconut and nut topping is a tasty addition.

Pumpkin Cookies

1 cup brown sugar
1 cup shortening
1 egg
1 cup pumpkin
1 teaspoon cinnamon
1 teaspoon baking powder
1 teaspoon baking soda
½ teaspoon salt
2 cups flour

Frosting
1 teaspoon butter
1 Tablespoon milk
¼ cup pumpkin
Add powdered sugar until thick enough to spread.

Cream together sugar, shortening and egg.
Add pumpkin, mix well.
Add dry ingredients to mixture. Beat well.
Drop by rounded teaspoons on greased cookie sheet. Flatten a bit.
Bake at 350 degrees for 10-12 minutes.
When cookies are cool, spread on frosting.

Makes approximately 3 ½ dozen cookies.

This is a soft, flavorful cookie that is great to serve in the fall. They go well with hot tea or spiced cider. (Recipe on page 36)

Cooking Tips

Allow time for butter, margarine or cream cheese to become room temperature before using them in baked goods.

Determination

A sister and brother and their spouses from the Netherlands happened upon Peaceful Acres one day. After walking around the grounds, they decided they wanted to stay here and nowhere else! However, I was gone for the day so they continually tried to reach me by phone. I finally answered around 4 o'clock in the afternoon so they booked two rooms for two nights. They said they planned to continue calling me until rather late in the evening before they would have reserved rooms elsewhere. They were delightful people and the other guests enjoyed their sharing. Leslie, another guest, was celebrating a birthday so we sang "Happy Birthday" as I served her a muffin topped with a lit birthday candle as is the Peaceful Acres tradition. Then these two couples sang "Happy Birthday" to her in Dutch. That was very special to Leslie and will be a birthday she remembers for a long time.

Thoughtful Guests

A year earlier Judy had stopped in to tour Peaceful Acres to see if she might want to have their annual sister gathering here sometime. She decided that she would reserve our rooms for the following year. She was excited about spending time with her sisters, shopping in Shipshewana and attending the Chonda Pierce concert at the Convention Center. They had a great time together but the one sister had to leave for home before the concert. The others insisted that I use her ticket and go to the concert with them at no cost to me! What a thoughtful gesture. We all enjoyed the evening together.

Thoughtful Guests 2

As I recall, Dot emailed me from their winter getaway in Arizona asking if I could accommodate four ladies from their quilting group, "The Cut-Ups," during the week of the quilt festival in Shipshewana. I was pleased to take their reservation and have enjoyed their company during that week for three years now. Their name not only depicts what they enjoy doing but it also describes their personalities! They have always connected so well with the other guests and I remember several times how warmly they included some guests who were here by themselves. In fact, last year they met one of the guests downtown and invited her to eat lunch with them.

A highlight of their visit here is when they gather around the family room in the evening for their nightly "Show and Tell" time. Everyone shares the patterns, fabrics and other things they bought that day. That is also a time when ideas are freely shared and copied for future reference. During one of those sharing times, my son called to check if we were listening to the radio or TV. When I told him, "No," he advised that we go to the basement immediately as there was a tornado warning in our area. The show and tell time continued downstairs with a bit of anxiousness expressed now and then. However, one guest said she really enjoys storms and went out on the front porch to watch it! After a while, I thought she was certainly staying outside a long time so I came upstairs to check on her just as my phone rang. It was her calling because she had locked herself out. I was concerned that she had to stay outside so long but she enjoyed it!

They also have fun putting puzzles together. Last summer a couple of ladies wanted to complete the puzzle that was started so they stayed up until 1:00 AM to do so. Then they bought me a new puzzle to add to my collection!

To add to their thoughtfulness, The Cut-Ups have showered me with gifts of their lovely handiwork. One summer I mentioned that I didn't really use one set of antique china very often because I didn't have anything to go with it. Josie immediately wrote down the colors of the flowers in the china and the next summer they brought me lovely quilted placemats that were a great match for the china. They had also made me a beautiful lap quilt with Bible verses written around the border. They had all signed their names on a heart shape on back of the quilt that has this verse written on it. "Dearest Friend, May your joys be deep as the ocean and your sorrows as light as it's foam. Live peacefully." The quilt was in a reversible quilted bag that I have found useful for carrying many different things. Their other gift was an accordion file box holding many of their favorite recipes they had copied for me. I have enjoyed trying out the recipes and use some of them regularly. I told them it seemed like Christmas! Their gifts and friendship have meant a lot to me. I look forward to their visit again this summer.

From the Guestbook . . .

"I have stayed in a variety of Bed and Breakfasts and this is definitely one of the best. What a wonderful retreat!"

Thoughtful Guests 3

Through the years, I have appreciated many thoughtful gifts from guests like Carmen and Amy. The two of them have been friends for many years and they love to travel together to the flea market in Shipshewana. They come here at least once or twice a summer. A few summers ago they had fun finding some accessories for Amy's daughter's wedding, which took place later that summer. Carmen loves to crochet and she has given me dishcloths she made while she was here. She has also sent me some in the mail, as well as a beautiful crocheted scarf which I enjoy wearing. Last year Amy brought napkin rings to match those I use frequently because she knew I had been hunting for more. The napkin rings have a little section to put cut flowers in and a section for the napkin. I was so pleased to have more of them. She found them at a garage sale but they were still in their original packaging! There was also a salt and pepper unit to match them! When I served a retirement tea on the front porch last summer, I was so glad for the extra ones. I had just enough after I figured out how to tape the holes closed on the salt and pepper unit so it would hold water. I really enjoy Carmen and Amy's regular visits to Peaceful Acres.

Thoughtful Guests 4

It was springtime when Dory, her mother Pauline and her Aunt Doris visited Peaceful Acres. They were all thrilled that Dory was pregnant and would give birth to a baby girl that summer. When baby Kaitlyn was three months old, Dory and her husband, Micah, brought her to Peaceful Acres for a visit. What a sweetheart!

I will always remember that particular visit because "somehow" we got on the subject of health concerns and I shared with them that I was anxious about a medical procedure that I was having done in a few days. Micah and Dory immediately suggested that we have prayer together concerning that procedure. Their prayers were so sweet and sincere and definitely had a calming effect on me.

On one of their visits, they brought Dory's father and stepmother as their guests. Again, "somehow" it was mentioned that my pickup truck wouldn't start so Micah and his father-in-law decided to use the jumper cables on it. However, they discovered that it needed a new battery so they insisted on going downtown to buy a new battery and then replaced it for me. What a gift! God knew just when to send them to me!

They have visited on various occasions and it always seems that they can detect just what I need. Micah shoveled the snowy front walks on their last visit. Their heart for God and giving spirits probably explains why they are in ministry.

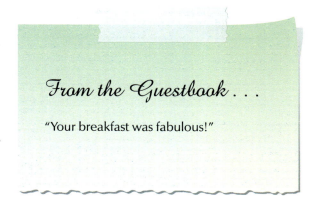

From the Guestbook . . .

"Your breakfast was fabulous!"

Thoughtful Guests 5

Joan and Russ had traveled to the East from California to visit Joan's father in a nursing home and decided to spend several days in Shipshewana to get away from their fast-paced lives. They ate breakfast one morning with people who shared deeply about their joys and struggles in life. In fact, the guests all wrote down their names and email addresses and asked me to make a copy for each one so they could stay in touch. Russ and Joan attended church services with me on Sunday morning and commented that they would like to find a Mennonite Church in their area. Joan is a Kindergarten teacher in an inner-city school so Russ assists in her classroom since he has retired from the military.

A few weeks after their departure, my mail included a Beverly Lewis book from Joan and Russ. I was surprised but after doing some checking, I realized that it was one I didn't have on my bookshelf. Unbeknownst to me, they must have looked through my Beverly Lewis novels and noted that this particular one was missing in a series. This is just one more example of people's thoughtfulness.

Thoughtful Guests 6

I was cutting fabric for tablecloth overlays when Sue and Renee arrived. When I found out that Sue was an accomplished quilter, I asked her for advice in hemming the cloths. She advised that I use iron-on tape to make a nice finish on them. I thought that was a good idea and was planning to go downtown to buy the tape at one of our well-known fabric/sewing centers. However, the two ladies insisted on going downtown to pick it up for me. I argued that I preferred to have it soon so I could continue working on them but they said they would bring it back for me! They were such a blessing to me on that heavily scheduled, busy day.

These stories highlight only a few of our "Thoughtful Guests." Many have invited me to join them for dinner, brought lovely flowers and plants, CD's, cookbooks from their home areas and other mementoes. One lady even gave me a foot massage. But best of all they have brought their friendship and prayers. I have concluded that people who frequent Bed and Breakfasts are a very unique, special group of people!

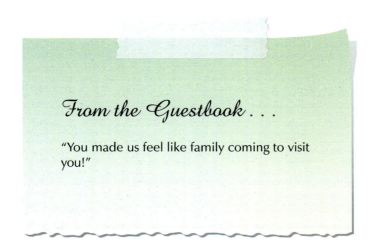

From the Guestbook . . .

"You made us feel like family coming to visit you!"

Vows Renewed

As it happens occasionally when guests forget that Indiana is on Eastern time, the phone rang late one night. I sleepily answered to hear Glenda explain that she and her husband Doug were celebrating their 30th anniversary in June. She was hoping to plan a very special surprise for him so she wanted to book the Garden Getaway Suite for two nights. Glenda questioned whether I knew of a place they could go to renew their marriage vows. I suggested that there would be several locations on the grounds of Peaceful Acres that would serve as a lovely setting for the ceremony. She decided that they would like to have it here. I invited my friends, a retired pastor and his wife, to join us on Tuesday evening to take charge of the renewal service.

Unknown to Glenda, the couple's daughter called me several days later. She was excited about her mother's plans and explained that she and her brothers and sisters wanted to be part of the celebration so they were planning to make the two and one half hour's drive to surprise their parents.

On Tuesday evening at exactly 6:00 with recorded music playing softly on the front porch, I rang the iron dinner bell six times. That was the signal for the family, who were in hiding in back of the house, to appear. Glenda and Doug, the pastor couple and I walked the flower-lined path to the gazebo. Glenda gasped as she turned to see their children and grandchildren walking across the lawn toward the gazebo. Doug commented later that he thought she must have spied a huge insect! With smiles and tears, they renewed their vows in the presence of their family. It turned out to be a very sentimental occasion. I felt so privileged to be part of this special celebration knowing that keeping one's marriage vibrant is so important. The couple was doing a great job of modeling this for their children and grandchildren.

Everyone enjoyed the punch and cookies served on the side porch following the ceremony. Doug wrote these comments in the guest book: "Thank you again for all your efforts in coordinating our renewal of vows. It was quite the surprise for me! Glenda and I were both floored by the arrival of the wedding guests."

It was another truly memorable day at Peaceful Acres!

Entrees

Biscuits with Sausage - Apple Gravy

6	frozen buttermilk biscuits (or use biscuit recipe on page 64)	3	Tablespoons flour
2	teaspoons butter or margarine	2¼	cups milk
2	medium apples, cored, chopped (about 1 ¼ cups)	½	teaspoon onion salt
1	pound bulk pork sausage	⅛	teaspoon black pepper

6   frozen buttermilk biscuits (or use biscuit recipe on page 64)

2   teaspoons butter or margarine

2   medium apples, cored, chopped (about 1 ¼ cups)

1   pound bulk pork sausage

3   Tablespoons flour

2¼ cups milk

½   teaspoon onion salt

⅛   teaspoon black pepper
      Dash of red pepper (cayenne)
      or sprinkle with paprika
      (optional)

Bake the biscuits.

Melt butter over medium heat in a 10-inch nonstick skillet.

Add apple pieces and cook 4-7 minutes until fairly tender.

In another skillet, brown sausage 4-6 minutes, stirring frequently, until no longer pink.

Add 1 Tablespoon flour, stirring constantly, until brown.

Stir in remaining flour.

Stir in milk with wire whisk.

Cook about 3 minutes, stirring constantly, until mixture thickens.

Stir in apple pieces, onion salt and pepper.

Split warm biscuits and top with sausage-apple gravy.

Serves 6.

I bake biscuits and brown sausage ahead of time so that this recipe doesn't take too long in the morning. If fact, I sometimes make the gravy the night before, refrigerate it and reheat it the next morning. For those who are not a fan of biscuits and gravy of which I was not, the apples really add a nice touch and new flavor. I enjoy this recipe. Don't peel the apples so you will retain more nutrients and add color to the gravy.

Baked Oatmeal

½ cup applesauce, oil or a stick of margarine (for a healthier dish, I use the applesauce.)
1 cup brown sugar
2 eggs
1 Tablespoon baking powder
1 cup milk

3 cups regular oatmeal
1 teaspoon salt
½ teaspoon ground cinnamon
⅔ cup chopped apple
½ cup peaches or blueberries (fresh or frozen)

Mix applesauce, sugar and eggs together.
Add remaining ingredients and stir until mixed.
Grease 9" x 11" pan (or 8" x 8").
Pour into greased pan and sprinkle with cinnamon.
Bake at 350 degrees for 30 minutes.

Serve with milk, brown sugar and a choice of dried fruits such as raisins or cranberries.

I find that most guests have never heard of baked oatmeal but they really like it. This is so handy to mix up the night before and bake in the morning. I often serve this on Sunday mornings as it saves time on a busy morning when you are getting ready to leave for church.

Amish Scramble

1   pound fresh, smoked sausage
6   eggs
2½ cups milk
1   Tablespoon dry mustard
2   cups shredded cheddar cheese
8-10 slices bread (I use leftover French bread or rolls and a mixture of
      white and whole wheat breads.)
      Salt and pepper to taste
1   can mushroom soup
½   cup milk

Precook and drain sausage.
Beat the eggs with milk and dry mustard.
Cube the bread and put in greased 9" x 13" pan.
Layer meat, egg mixture and cheese.
Cover and refrigerate overnight.
In the morning, mix soup with ½ cup milk.
Pour over bread mixture.
Bake uncovered at 350 degrees for 1 hour.
Remove from oven and let set 5 minutes before cutting and serving.

Serves 8.

*This is a good way to use up the ends of the French bread you used to make
French toast. Be sure to bake uncovered!*

Blueberry French Toast

8 cups cubed day-old white bread, crusts removed (I usually use French or Vienna bread and some whole wheat)
1 – 8 ounce package cream cheese
1 cup fresh or frozen blueberries
10 eggs
2 cups milk
1/3 cup maple syrup or honey

Cut bread into 1-inch cubes.
Place half in greased 9" x 13" pan.
Cut cream cheese into very small cubes and distribute over bread.
Top with blueberries and remaining bread.
Beat eggs, milk and syrup together and pour over bread.
Cover and refrigerate overnight.
Bake covered at 350 degrees for 30 minutes – uncover, bake 30 minutes more.

Sauce

1 cup sugar
2 Tablespoons cornstarch
1 cup water
1 Tablespoon butter
3/4 – 1 cup blueberries

Combine sugar and cornstarch; add water
Bring to boil – boil for 3 minutes, stirring constantly.
Stir in blueberries.
Simmer for 8-10 minutes.

Makes 10-12 servings.

Serve warm sauce over toast. Delicious!

Breakfast Pizza

1 - 8 ounce package refrigerated crescent rolls (8 rolls) spread out in 9" x 13" greased pan or if you want to cut it in wedge-shaped pieces, use 1½ - 8 ounce (12) crescent rolls spread out on 12" greased pizza pan. Be sure to seal the perforations completely.

½ pound sausage
½ cup chopped onion
1 cup cheddar cheese
2 Tablespoons green pepper

4 eggs, lightly beaten
½ teaspoon salt
1 teaspoon oregano
⅛ teaspoon pepper
¾ cup milk

Brown sausage and onion together.
Sprinkle over dough.
Sprinkle cheese and green pepper over meat layer.
Blend remainder of ingredients and pour over the entire pizza.
Top with 1 cup mozzarella cheese.
Bake at 350 degrees for 25 minutes.

Serves 8.

Don't forget to have the 1 cup mozzarella cheese available for the top!
For a 12" pizza pan, I use only 3 eggs and ½ cup milk so it doesn't bake over the sides. The light crust makes this a delicious breakfast entrée.

Breakfast Tortillas

Small round corn or flour tortillas (cut off ½ to 1 inch around edge)
Fit into greased muffin tins.
Fill with ¼ cup black beans or refried beans mixed with 1 Tablespoon of salsa of choice.
Add whole egg on top of beans or scrambled eggs with cheese, onions, peppers, hash browns, sausage, cilantro, green chilies and salt and pepper. (whatever you choose to add)
Fill the tortilla at least to the top of muffin cup.
Bake at 350 degrees for approximately 8 minutes or until tortilla is slightly browned on the edges.
Sprinkle Pepper Jack Cheese (or cheese of your choice) on top of each tortilla.
Then cover the whole pan with foil and bake 5 more minutes.

Serve with salsa and sour cream.

These tortillas take on a southwest flavor if you add cilantro and green chilies. If you scramble your eggs, don't let them get dry and overdone. I prefer the refried beans on the bottom but others may like the black bean option. I make my egg mixture the night before so it isn't so time consuming in the morning. Be creative and try them different ways.

Delicious Baked Eggs

1	cup Bisquick mix	6	eggs, slightly beaten
1½	cups cottage cheese	1	cup milk
2	cups grated cheddar cheese	5	Tablespoons butter
2	teaspoons minced onion or onion flakes		

Mix and stir in order given except for butter.
Melt butter in 9″ x 13″ or 6″ x 10″ pan.
Add above mixture.
Mix butter into the egg mixture.
Bake at 350 degrees for 40 minutes.
Cool several minutes before cutting into squares.

Serves 6-8 people

Eggs Florentine

Add 1 cup fresh or frozen chopped spinach to above mixture.

Both recipes are delicious served with sausage links or slices of ham.

Cooking Tips

Substitute whipped up cottage cheese (in the blender) if you are out of sour cream.

Gourmet Brunch Cups

12 puff pastry shells
6 oz. bulk sausage
1 cup sour cream
6 ounces shredded Monterey
   Jack cheese
¼ cup Parmesan cheese
1 egg, beaten
2 Tablespoons flour

2 Tablespoons milk (I usually add
   more
3 green onions, chopped
½ teaspoon dried basil
1 teaspoon prepared mustard
1 teaspoon paprika
1 teaspoon parsley

Bake shells as directed on package, take off caps, remove dough center.
Cook sausage, drain.
Combine all ingredients.
Pack shells with mixture.
Sprinkle with paprika.
Bake at 325 degrees for 30-40 minutes.
Garnish with caps and parsley.

These brunch cups are good for breakfast or when serving a brunch or tea.
They are unique and make a nice presentation.

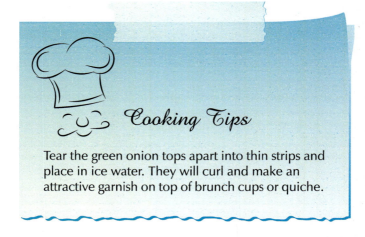

Cooking Tips

Tear the green onion tops apart into thin strips and
place in ice water. They will curl and make an
attractive garnish on top of brunch cups or quiche.

French Toast in a Bowl

4	cups cubed whole wheat bread	¼	cup butter or margarine
½	cup raisins, or dried cherries, or cranberries (or a combination)	½	cup sugar
		2	eggs, beaten
		½	teaspoon nutmeg or cinnamon
1½	cups milk	⅛	teaspoon salt
		1	teaspoon vanilla

In a large bowl combine bread and raisins.
In a 1-quart saucepan combine milk and butter.
Warm to melt butter over medium heat, 3-5 minutes.
Pour milk over bread and dried fruit. Let stand 10 minutes.
Add sugar, eggs, nutmeg, salt and vanilla.
Stir well and pour into greased 1 ½ quart casserole.
Sprinkle with nutmeg or cinnamon.
Bake at 350 degrees for 40 to 50 minutes or until center is set.
Serve with warm maple syrup.

Serves 4

I use a combination of whole wheat or white breads and rolls for the 4 cups of bread. I usually mix this the night before and refrigerate overnight. If it has been refrigerated, it takes approximately 1 hour to bake. This recipe was shared with me by a guest and has been enjoyed and copied by many other guests.

Gingerbread Pancakes

2½ cups flour
5 teaspoons baking powder
1½ teaspoons salt
1 teaspoon baking soda
1 teaspoon cinnamon
½ teaspoon ginger

¼ cup molasses
2 cups milk
2 eggs
6 Tablespoons butter, melted
1 cup raisins (optional)

Stir together the flour, baking powder, salt, baking soda and spices.
In a separate bowl combine the molasses and milk; beat in the eggs and the melted butter.
Add to the flour mixture and stir until just moistened; stir in the raisins.
Ladle the batter onto a hot, lightly oiled griddle and cook until golden on both sides.
Serve hot, with butter and maple syrup.

Makes 8 large pancakes.

I don't serve pancakes very often but will choose them for the menu when there are children among the guests. To make a teddy bear shape for the children, I add ears from the batter and chocolate chips or raisins to make the eyes, nose and mouth. Both adults and children enjoy these pancakes.

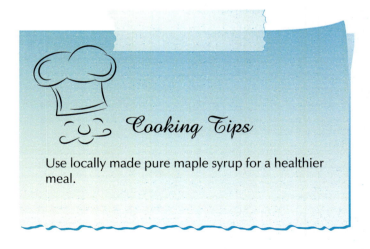

Cooking Tips

Use locally made pure maple syrup for a healthier meal.

Harvest Vegetable Frittata

2 Tablespoons butter	½ cup water
½ pound mushrooms, sliced	2 Tablespoons mustard
1 cup diced zucchini	¼ teaspoon pepper
½ cup chopped green pepper	½ teaspoon salt
¼ cup chopped onion	1 cup shredded cheese (variety
1 tomato, diced	of your choice)
4 eggs (or more)	Paprika to taste

Melt butter in large skillet.
Add mushrooms, zucchini, green pepper and onion.
Cook over medium heat for 6 minutes, stirring occasionally.
Add tomato.
Lightly beat together eggs, water, salt, pepper and mustard.
Pour over vegetables in skillet.
Cook covered over medium heat for 5 – 10 minutes.
Sprinkle with cheese and paprika.
Cut into wedges.

Makes 8 slices.

This is another recipe for which you can pick and choose what you want to include. Shredded carrots, spinach or asparagus could be added. I don't usually add mushrooms as many people are like me and would just as soon do without them! I recall making an individual frittata for a guest who was lactose intolerant. I just skipped the cheese and used a bit of olive oil instead of butter. She considered it a very special breakfast and was quite pleased.

Morning Mix-Up

2   Tablespoons vegetable oil
2   cups frozen hash browns
1   cup chopped cooked ham
¼   cup chopped green peppers
½   cup chopped onion
6-8 eggs

2   teaspoons dry mustard
    Salt and pepper to taste
1   cup shredded cheddar cheese
    Minced fresh chives or parsley
    (optional)

Sauté potatoes, ham, peppers and onion in oil for 10 minutes or until potatoes are tender.
Beat together eggs, mustard, salt and pepper.
Add to the skillet; cook, stirring occasionally, until eggs are set.
Remove from heat and gently stir in cheese.
Spoon onto serving platter or make individual servings with a large scoop.
Sprinkle with chives or parsley.

Serves 5.

I keep chopped ham frozen in 1 cup amounts in the freezer. This saves time in the morning when making any recipe that calls for chopped ham. This is a good recipe to make for just a few people because it is so easy to vary the amounts. I usually figure two eggs per person and include veggies of any amount I choose!

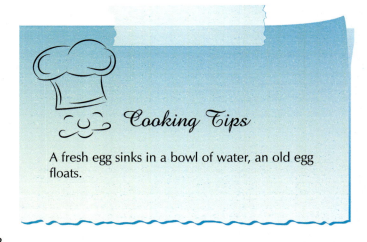

Cooking Tips

A fresh egg sinks in a bowl of water, an old egg floats.

Oven Baked Praline French Toast

8 slices French bread cut ¾ inch thick	½ teaspoon vanilla
6 eggs	½ teaspoon nutmeg
1 cup half and half or milk	⅛ teaspoon salt
2 Tablespoons sugar	⅓ cup plus 1 Tablespoon butter
2 Tablespoons orange juice	½ cup chopped pecans
	¼ cup light brown sugar

Place bread in single layer in 9" x 13" glass baking dish.
Blend together eggs, milk, sugar, orange juice, vanilla, nutmeg and salt.
Pour over bread, turning once to coat evenly.
Refrigerate, covered, several hours or overnight.
Place ⅓ cup butter in jellyroll pan or glass baking dish. Melt butter in oven-distribute evenly.
Arrange soaked bread in single layer in butter-coated pan.
Bake uncovered at 375 degrees approximately 25 minutes or until firm or golden brown.
Melt 1 Tablespoon butter and mix with pecans and brown sugar.
Sprinkle over baked French toast.
Return to oven 5 minutes or until sugar starts to bubble.
Serve with maple syrup.

Serves 8.

This nutty toast is a nice variation of French toast especially if your other courses are fruit based. Quite tasty!

Overnight Apple French Toast

1 cup packed brown sugar
½ cup butter or margarine
2 Tablespoons light corn syrup
2 large tart apples, peeled and sliced ¼ inch thick (I slice them thinner!)

3 eggs
1 cup milk
1 teaspoon vanilla
9 slices day-old French bread (sliced ¾ inch thick)

Cook brown sugar, butter and corn syrup until thick, about 5-7 minutes.
Pour into ungreased 9" x 13" pan.
Arrange apples on top.
Beat eggs, milk and vanilla.
Dip bread into egg mixture for 1 minute.
Place over apples.
Sprinkle with cinnamon.
Cover and refrigerate overnight.
Remove from refrigerator 30 minutes before baking.
Bake uncovered at 350 degrees for 35-40 minutes.

Syrup (optional)

1 cup applesauce
1-10 ounce jar apple jelly
½ teaspoon cinnamon
⅛ teaspoon cloves

Combine syrup ingredients in a medium saucepan.
Cook and stir until hot.
Serve over French toast.

I stopped making the syrup because people didn't use it. The syrup at the bottom of the baking pan adds enough liquid and sweetness.

Apple French toast is another Peaceful Acres favorite. It is hearty and scrumptious!

Peach Kuchen

¾ cup whole wheat flour
½ cup white flour
2 Tablespoons sugar
¼ teaspoon salt
¼ teaspoon baking powder
¼ cup ground walnuts (optional)
Combine above ingredients in a large bowl.

¼ cup butter
Cut butter into above ingredients until crumbly. Pat mixture over bottom and sides of a 9" pie pan.

4 cups peeled, fresh or canned peaches.
Place sliced peaches in pastry.

3 Tablespoons sugar
1 teaspoon ground cinnamon.
Mix together and sprinkle on top. Bake in preheated oven at 400 degrees for 15 minutes.

1 cup plain yogurt or sour cream
1 egg, beaten
2 Tablespoons sugar
½ teaspoon vanilla
Combine and pour over peaches and bake 30 minutes longer or until set.

Serves 6-8

"Kuchen" is the German word for cake. This kuchen isn't very sweet and can be served with ham or sausages as part of the main course or serve it as a breakfast dessert. You can substitute 3 cups blueberries for the peaches if you prefer! I have made it with half peaches and half blueberries. . . delicious!

Sausage Quiche

½ pound sausage (or use hamburger if you prefer)
½ cup mayonnaise (I use a bit less)
½ cup milk
3 eggs
1 Tablespoon cornstarch

1 cup shredded Cheddar cheese
⅓ cup sliced green onions (or use regular onions, minced)
2 Tablespoons chopped green pepper
2 Tablespoons chopped ripe olives.

Brown meat and drain fat.
Blend mayonnaise, milk, beaten eggs and cornstarch.
Stir in meat, cheese, onion, green pepper and olives.

Pour into unbaked 9" pie shell.
Bake at 350 degrees for 40 minutes or until set.

Serves 6-8.

I also sprinkle some extra cheese over the top.

A gracious teaching colleague brought this quiche to our family many years ago after I had surgery. We enjoyed it so this has become a "go to" recipe ever since that time. It is a quick, easy recipe and works well for breakfast, brunch or lunch. I keep browned sausage and piecrusts in the freezer as a time saver when a recipe calls for those items.

I am adding Grandma Kreider's pie crust recipe at the request of my daughter. It is easy to make and always turns out well. They also freeze well.

Grandma Kreider's Pie Crust

3   cups flour
1¼ cup shortening
2   teaspoons salt
1   Tablespoon sugar

1   egg
½   cup water
1   Tablespoon vinegar

Mix first four ingredients with a pastry blender.
Beat the egg. Add water and vinegar and mix well.
Mix liquid ingredients into dry ingredients.

Chill before rolling into pie shells or keep dough in the refrigerator up to a week.

Makes 4 to 5 crusts

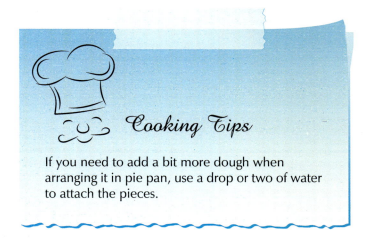

Cooking Tips

If you need to add a bit more dough when arranging it in pie pan, use a drop or two of water to attach the pieces.

Spinach Sensation Quiche

½ pound bacon slices (I use less)
1 cup (8 ounces) sour cream
3 eggs, separated
2 Tablespoons flour
⅛ teaspoon black pepper
1 package (10 ounces) frozen chopped spinach, thawed and squeezed dry

½ cup (2 ounces) shredded sharp Cheddar cheese
½ cup dry bread crumbs
1 Tablespoon butter, melted

Serves 6-8.

Spray 2-quart round baking dish with nonstick cooking spray.

Prepare bacon, crumble and set aside.

Combine sour cream, egg yolks, flour and pepper in large bowl; set aside.
Beat egg whites in medium bowl with mixer at high speed until stiff peaks form. Stir ¼ of egg whites into sour cream mixture; fold in remaining egg whites.

Arrange half of spinach in prepared dish. Top with half of the sour cream mixture. Sprinkle ¼ cup cheese over sour cream mixture. Sprinkle bacon over cheese. Repeat layers, ending with remaining ¼ cup cheese.

Combine bread crumbs and butter in small bowl; sprinkle evenly over cheese. These crumbs really add flavor to the quiche.

Bake, uncovered, at 350 degrees for 30 to 35 minutes or until egg mixture is set. Let stand five minutes before serving.

This is a light quiche that seems to be enjoyed by all. Sometimes I hesitate making it without asking if the guests like spinach but most people do. You can have the bacon fried and crumbled ahead of time. I think many weight-watchers appreciate that it doesn't have a crust. Serve with fruit and muffins.

Stuffed Apricot French Toast

Filling:
8   ounces cream cheese, softened
1   teaspoon vanilla
2   Tablespoons apricot preserves
½ cup chopped nuts

1½ pounds French or Vienna bread
4   eggs
½ teaspoon vanilla
1   cup milk
12 ounce jar apricot preserves
½ cup orange juice

Beat cream cheese and 1 teaspoon vanilla until fluffy.
Add 2 Tablespoons preserves.
Stir in nuts. Set aside.

Cut bread into slices approximately ½ inch thick.
Make a sandwich with the cream cheese mixture between two slices of bread.
Mix together eggs, vanilla and milk.
Dip both sides of sandwich in egg mixture.
Brown both sides in frying pan.
Place on ungreased baking sheet.
Bake at 300 degrees for 20 minutes.
Combine remaining preserves and orange juice. Heat
Drizzle over French toast before serving.

Makes 6-8 servings.

This has been a favorite throughout the years of hosting bed and breakfast guests. I sometimes just completely finish the toast in the pan on top of the stove rather than putting it in the oven. However, it you do put it in the oven, you don't have to watch it as closely!

Predicted Nuptials

When I greeted Jan and Bob at the front door, I noticed there was quite a big difference in their ages, but I was not aware of how much difference and it wasn't important to me.

However, the next morning at breakfast Bob commented, "Jan, why don't you tell Mary Jane our story." And so their amazing love story unfolded. Jan was just a little girl when she visited her young cousin and her family in Washington, D.C. They were privileged to attend a concert presented by the U. S. Air Force Choir. Sitting close to the front of the auditorium, the little girls listened and giggled about the handsome tenor soloist who had a noticeable space between his front teeth. Jan flippantly told her cousin that she would marry that man some day and her cousin replied, "He probably whistles when he talks because of the space between his front teeth!"

Many years passed by and both Jan and the young soloist went on to pursue careers in the field of music. Jan taught music in the states and the tenor soloist pursued his singing career in Germany. However, after some years, Bob moved back to the states and became a college music professor and voice teacher. Eventually Jan decided to study voice again and as fate would have it, Bob was her teacher. However, they had no idea that they had ever seen each other before. The professor had since had his teeth corrected or that would have been the tell tale sign! As the two began getting to know each other better, it suddenly occurred to Jan one day who this professor might be! She asked if he had sung in the Air Force choir at a concert in Washington, D.C. in a certain year. His answer was, yes, he was the tenor soloist who sang at the concert that very night that Jan and her cousin attended. After some time, they began dating and ultimately married. The happy pair believes that only the Lord could have orchestrated their meeting again.

One of the rewards of running a bed and breakfast is having people share their unique stories with you. One's world is broadened as your circle of friends is expanded.

Sermon: John 14:2

Pastor Ken and wife Bev, who come from a warm southwestern state where people like to go to retire, decided they would like to reverse that tradition and retire in Shipshewana, Indiana ! They had lived in Indiana for a time and fell in love with the countryside and people of Shipshewana. They travel to this area fairly frequently to look for land or tour houses for sale, to meet with builders and cabinetmakers and other construction experts. They enjoyed their restful time at Peaceful Acres putting together almost all of a 1,000 piece puzzle and enjoying the paths and gardens here.

Upon their return home, Pastor Ken sent me a copy of a sermon he had preached at their church. It was based on John 14. His last point was from verse 2, "I go to prepare a place for you." He wrote:

> "Some see those words from a human standpoint, that Jesus is preparing as we would prepare when we're having guests.
> At Shipshewana's Country Hideaway, Peaceful Acres Bed and Breakfast, our hostess Mary Jane had prepared a place for Bev and me, all right. She had placed empty hangers for all our things on shaker pegs on a simple shelf rack that hung between two over-sized windows from which soft candlelight streamed. Homemade soap "rose petals" sat beside clean towels at the sink. A colorful, hand-stitched quilt covered the queen-sized bed frame, stretching from the handsome, Amish-made wooden headboard to footboard. One of several books thoughtfully stacked up on the nightstand offered, "101 Things to Do in Shipshewana." In a tasteful binder we discovered many different restaurant menus for meals our hostess considered we might enjoy later in the day, long after our delicately, gourmet three-course breakfasts had worn off.
> If those are just some of the personal touches Mary Jane goes through to prepare for her guests, who knows what

our Heavenly Host's preparations for our rooms in the heavenly Bed and Breakfast might entail. We could guess; but, even better, we could leave it at this: Jesus' presence – His "touches," in a literal sense – is what will make the "mansions" or "rooms" in our "Father's house" ready for us. For only "through the presence of our Redeemer in heaven is it possible for us disciples to enter heaven."

I appreciated all the little things that Pastor Ken noticed and remembered. However, it is a pale comparison to the preparations that our Lord is making for us.

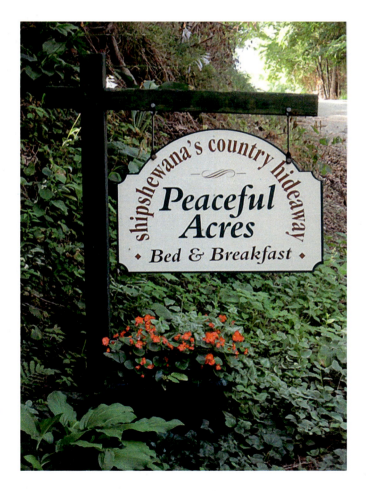

Shared Interests

Brad and Elaine were celebrating their first anniversary. Ted and Kim were on a getaway to choose a name for their first child due to arrive in three months. When the two couples met, they quickly discovered that they were both involved as worship leaders in their respective churches.

It was a lovely warm July evening so the foursome sat out on the wraparound porch until after 11:00 PM sharing music ideas and many other things they found they had in common. As the fireflies lit up the night sky, sounds of laughter and joy drifted into the night atmosphere. Later, Brad commented, "This is just the way a Bed and Breakfast is supposed to be according to the movie, "Groundhog Day." I had never seen that movie so I watched it sometime later. I hope he was referring only to the fact that the story took place in a Bed and Breakfast! Both couples were so grateful that God had planned for them to come to Peaceful Acres at the same time. It was His divine plan!

What a lovely spot

We have so much enjoyed our stay!

The Tuba Man

Larry and his mother, Louetta, have come to Peaceful Acres for a mother/son get-away for six years now. Each time, Larry brings his tuba to entertain us at breakfast or during the evening hours. He is an accomplished musician and sometimes also provides us with piano music or with songs on his harmonica. One still, summer evening he played for a long time down in the garden area among the flowers and vegetables. The next day, some neighbors mentioned that they really enjoyed hearing the music the evening before.

We have become good friends through the years. In fact, it is their family who took my cat, Smokey, to join their family. (his tale is told in the story called, "Feline Lovers".) Smokey gets along just fine with their resident cat appropriately named Tuba. I remember the time that Larry and Louetta visited right after the death and funeral of Louetta's mother. It was a good time to reminiscence with them and share their sense of pain and loss. I also look forward to hearing about Larry's latest adventures and accomplishments in the world of music. They enjoy visiting the music store in the Davis Mercantile Building down town and usually find music treasures they can't resist buying.

After their mother/son get away last summer, Louetta brought her former boss and good friend from Florida to visit Peaceful Acres. Since it was her friend's birthday, she brought a birthday cake and ice cream to celebrate. I was privileged to join them for this special celebration.

I sometimes question if they wouldn't enjoy trying another Bed and Breakfast for their annual getaway but I'm pleased that they continue to make reservations at Peaceful Acres. I'm looking forward to seeing them again this year.

Honeymooners

I opened the door to find a handsome young man with a captivating British accent. He explained that he was getting married later that summer and he would like to check out my rooms to possibly reserve one for their honeymoon. He mentioned that his fiancé was in the car. I asked if he didn't want to bring her in to which he replied, "Oh, no, the room must be a surprise!" He was soon enamored by our Garden Getaway Suite and reserved it for three nights.   About a week before their wedding date I received a call from the bride's sister asking if she and some friends could come to decorate the room that morning before the ceremony. The room looked lovely decorated with heart-shaped candles, little gifts of love, and rose petals scattered over the quilt, hot tub and floor.

The couple had told me they would probably arrive at Peaceful Acres at approximately 10:00 – 10:30 PM. That was a convenient time as I planned to be gone for the evening. I was pleased when I arrived home at 9 o'clock knowing that I would be home in plenty of time for their late arrival. However, as I drove in the lane, I saw their car parked in the parking area! They were sitting on the front porch blissfully awaiting my return! They asked me to take pictures of Brent carrying Kate over the threshold and some other pictures of them in their vintage wedding garb.

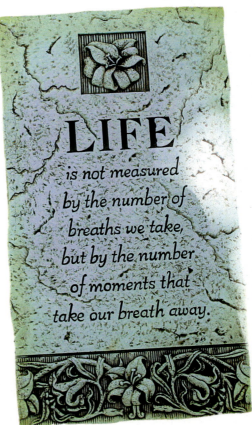

LIFE is not measured by the number of breaths we take, but by the number of moments that take our breath away.

How exciting to be part of the beginning of their new adventures as husband and wife!

One year later Brent and Kate came back to celebrate their first anniversary and they brought with them their darling baby girl. It was fun to catch up on their lives and to meet their first child.

Their next visit was also quite special as they brought Brent's parents who were visiting from England. However, the circumstances were not celebratory as were their first two visits. Brent's parents planned the trip to the United States to meet their second grandchild. However, instead they visited his gravesite. He died in utero at eight months gestation with no answers as to what went wrong. So the visit was bittersweet. The grandparents enjoyed spending time with their son and daughter-in-law and their little granddaughter but there was an underlying sadness. Their stay at Peaceful Acres was a time of much needed relaxation in peaceful surroundings. They did not understand God's ways but praised Him for His love and faithfulness.

On their honeymoon visit, they presented me with a lovely wooden magnet engraved with this verse from Psalm 23:6 "Goodness and mercy shall follow me all the days of my life, and I shall dwell in the house of the Lord forever." It is a special keepsake that I always keep on my refrigerator door.

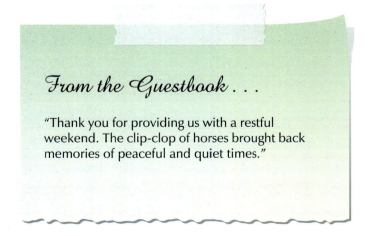

From the Guestbook . . .

"Thank you for providing us with a restful weekend. The clip-clop of horses brought back memories of peaceful and quiet times."

Making Rose Soap Petals

When we first moved to Peaceful Acres to open our Bed and Breakfast, I found a local person who made regular bar soaps and lovely rose-petal soaps for hand washing. I was fascinated with the rose petals and found that our guests enjoyed using them. However, the soap maker had other business matters to take care of and didn't continue making soaps very long! So I ordered rose petal soaps from the Internet. They weren't nearly as satisfactory as the homemade ones so I decided I would make them myself. I found that it wasn't too difficult and that I enjoyed making them. The one problem I encountered was that the glycerin always got a scum on top, which doesn't make a nice, clear petal if you cover it with scum! I searched the Internet for directions, asked others who had done it before and called a soap-making supply company for advice. No one was really able to answer the dilemma. Recently a dear friend helped me on soap making day. She discovered that if you don't use a double boiler in which to melt the glycerin but put the saucepan directly on the stove, it doesn't form the scum because the temperature remains hotter. However, one must be very careful as it burns quickly. Just in case you would like to try it, I have

included the instructions below! You might be able to perfect the process!

Buy silk rose petals of varying colors at a craft store.
Choose your fragrances according to the colors of your petals. For instance, I use a rose fragrance for the red petals, lavender or lilac for the purple ones and vanilla for the white petals.I could not find silk leaves that looked like leaves from a rose bush so I just buy cheap roses and cut off the leaves. (Garage sales are a good source!)

Melt the glycerin in a saucepan on top of double boiler (this does work if you stir the mixture each time before dipping the rose petal) or put the saucepan directly on the burner. Add the fragrance you choose and stir.

Use a long-nosed pliers or a tweezers to dip the rose petal in the mixture. Let drain on a cookie rack. Put wax paper underneath for easier cleanup.

They dry quickly and can be stored in plastic containers or bags.

The utensil you use for dipping does leave a small, uncovered spot on the petal so I often dip them again when I can handle them with my hands.

Enjoy using them! I package them and sell them to guests. They make really nice gifts for someone who has everything!

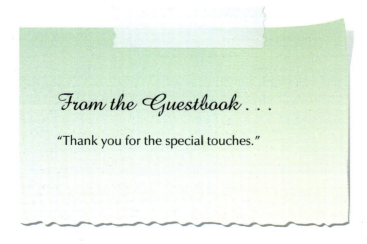

From the Guestbook . . .

"Thank you for the special touches."

Index